Trust
the Story

LaNette W. Thompson

ISBN: 978-0-9971956-1-3

Cover by Blake Kidney

Unless otherwise noted, all Scripture quotations are taken from the Holman Christian Standard Bible®, Used by Permission HCSB ©1999,2000,2002,2003,2009 Holman Bible Publishers. Holman Christian Standard Bible®, Holman CSB®, and HCSB® are federally registered trademarks of Holman Bible Publishers.

Scripture quotations marked (ESV) are from the ESV® Bible (The Holy Bible, English Standard Version®), copyright © 2001 by Crossway, a publishing ministry of Good News Publishers. Used by permission. All rights reserved.

Contents

Preface

Stories were a big part of my upbringing in central Virginia. My parents made sure my brothers and I understood the narratives passed down for generations, framing our understanding of what it meant to be a Rodgers. They also told me the story of salvation in Jesus Christ. The day I made that story my own, it changed my life forever.

And yet, I did not always trust the power of stories to change lives. As a cross-cultural theological educator and church planter in South America, my approach to the Bible was very literate-oriented. One day a conference leader challenged us to learn a Bible story by heart and tell it to the group. I choose the story in John 9 of the Blind Man. I worked hard in preparation. As I told the story, something incredible happened. It came alive to me as never before. I literally wept at the end, as the healed man worshipped the Lord he saw with his physical eyes for the very first time.

The Lord used that simple exercise to completely change how I viewed the role of biblical stories in evangelism and discipleship. I began to see how learning the stories brought me closer to my Savior. As I told them in a faithfully contextualized way, I began to see others respond to the gospel as never before. The Holy Spirit used the same salvation story that saved me to change the lives of others. And those who heard faithfully repeated the Word, multiplying results.

LaNette Thompson has seen firsthand the power of stories to change lives. As an early adopter of Chronological Bible Storying she pioneered efforts in West Africa to communicate the gospel to oral learners. Dr. Thompson has written extensively on the topic of global orality and its role in missiology. She is a popular conference speaker on the role of storying and teaching nonliterate adults. Her research interests led her to complete a Ph.D. in Educational Psychology from Baylor University in 2015.

The International Centre for Excellence in Leadership is honored to partner with Dr. Thompson in the publication of this book. Our hope is that it will inspire and equip you to share the powerful, life-changing story of the gospel.

Dr. Lloyd W. Rodgers
Director
International Centre for Excellence in Leadership
2015

"But the word is very near you. It is in your mouth and in your heart, so that you can do it."
Deuteronomy 30:14 ESV

"For we have heard for ourselves, and we know that this is indeed the Savior of the world."
John 4:42 ESV

Introduction

I remember the feel of the Chenille bedspread as I lay beside my grandmother during naptime, a preschooler resisting sleep, listening to her stories of teenage escapades. I remember sitting at her feet, listening to stories of faraway missionaries, as she led Women's Missionary Union lessons at our church. In Sunday School I heard Bible stories that established a foundation for my understanding of Christ and His love for me. Then I grew up and put away childish things like stories, or so I thought.

Intercultural communication and worldview interested me. I read the books recommended for missionaries going overseas. I learned about worldview and cultural anthropology through the writings of Kraft, Hiebert, Hesselgrave, and others. However, it was only after my husband and I were asked to pilot a chronological Bible storying project in West Africa that I learned the use of Bible stories as a cross-cultural witnessing tool.

As I struggled to learn the stories, I was forced to delve into Scripture as never before. When Jesus spoke to Peter after the walking-on-water incident, did Jesus say, "*Why* did you doubt?" or did He say, "Why did *you* doubt?" I will never forget the rapt faces of the African women as I told Bible stories, or being asked to repeat the story for a latecomer because "she has never heard." I saw the power of God's Word change lives as I shared Bible stories. And I asked myself, is there a reason why stories are so integral to evangelization and discipleship? I wanted to know more about how adults learn.

My quest led me to pursue an interdisciplinary master's degree. I designed my own degree, taking courses in history, anthropology, sociology, and cognitive psychology. I completed my thesis, *The Nonliterate and the Transfer of Knowledge in West Africa.* In my cognitive psychology courses, I learned about the importance of schemata in processing, storing, and interpreting information. I began to link the concepts of schemata and stories. Before, I had accepted Jesus' declaration that He would teach the crowds using parables - stories. Now I understood the reason behind His words. He had designed us and created us. He knew how we learned. Throughout my missionary career, I became more and more convinced of the power of stories and especially the stories in God's Word.

Following our retirement from the International Mission Board after 26 years, I completed a doctoral program in educational psychology, specializing in learning and development. As I studied theories that included the role of schemata in learning, I reflected on ways these learning theories had been demonstrated in my years of cross-cultural ministry. I considered the impact stories had had in my own personality development.

The purpose of this book is to share with you the fruits of my own study, personal experience, and insights into the ways in which God uses stories to change lives. I have included concepts I wish I had understood when I began my cross-cultural experience more than three decades ago. Stories are not just for children.

Part I provides the academic foundation of the book. I introduce the concepts of cognitive schemata, orality and literacy, intercultural communication, and learning. Those who specialize in these topics may cringe at my generalizations and argue with how I have linked schemata and stories. However, I believe that anyone who ministers cross-culturally, whether at home or abroad, will benefit from understanding these concepts.

Part II seeks to understand how the powerful cultural and familial stories in our lives have shaped us. Thinking critically about the stories that make us unique is vital to relationship-building and self-understanding. We reflect on the ways our personal stories and cultural values influence us as we seek to share a biblical worldview with others. Recognizing and sharing our faith stories gives the glory to God as He works in our lives.

In Part III, we look at various ways to share God's Word through the telling of Bible stories. This section is not meant to be an exhaustive training in contemporary methods but rather focuses on the necessity of being equipped. God may orchestrate a one-time encounter on an airplane or He may grant more time to share His Word with a neighbor. Either way, we want to be ready to faithfully tell the story of salvation.

Whether contemplating or just beginning a career overseas or living in the States and wondering how best to witness, this book will challenge you. Experienced cross-cultural workers will benefit from the emphasis on self-reflection in understanding themselves. Stories have power. Stories change lives. What is your story? What stories define you? "All Scripture is inspired by God and is profitable for teaching, for rebuking, for correcting, for training in righteousness, so that the man of God may be complete, equipped for every good work." (2 Timothy 3:16-17, HCSB). Do you know how to share God's story, His Word? Are you equipped to share your personal story of how God is working in your life?

PART I

What's so Powerful about Stories?

CHAPTER 1

Cognitive Schemata

Mark grasped Stacey's hand. Four years of college, three years of seminary, and five years of pastoring had all led up to this moment. He eyed the plaster walls of their tiny concrete house. Village sounds trickled in. He let go of Stacey and consulted his watch. Their language helper was already five minutes late. Leadership had told them in no uncertain terms that he and Stacey must learn the local language before they could begin ministry. More waiting....

Of Weddings and Horsetails...

I flipped through the clothes in my closet, searching for an outfit suitable to attend an African wedding. Our cultural informers, two young men studying to be Islamic teachers, had stopped by to inform my husband and me that several weddings were about to begin on main street in our village. I had attended Christian weddings at our previous assignment in a neighboring country. The brides had been dressed in white and slowly walked down the church aisle to the accompaniment of numerous singing bridesmaids. The ceremonies were similar to what I was used to in the United States, other than being about five-times longer. I had not yet attended a wedding in our Muslim village. I dressed excitedly. Our informers raised their eyes at my flowing embroidered robes when I emerged from the house, but they did not comment.

As we neared the village center, the rhythmic pounding of a drum was inescapable. I watched, my mouth open, as a scantily-clad bride appeared, balancing herself on the shoulders of her brother as he moved to the rhythm of the drum. In each hand, the young girl held a horsetail bound to a wooden stick, horsetails she swirled about her high in the air. An entourage of women, dancing to the pulsing of the drum and in rhythm with the bride's brother, encircled her. Small clouds of dust arose from their pounding feet. Soon another bride arrived from a different direction, twirling and balancing, her own group of women moving in harmony to the unique beat of their personal drummer. From different directions, more brides appeared. The street became packed with bridal groups, each with its own drummer, each group trying to out-dance the others. There were no grooms in sight. Our cultural informers pulled me away from the dust and swirling horsetails. Now, I understood why no one else was dressed as I was. My wedding schema had let me down.

What's In a Name?

In this chapter, we will examine how knowledge is created, organized, and stored as a type of story in our minds. We will also look at the impact these personal and cultural stories have on our behavior.

Imagine if every time you went to the grocery store, you had to rediscover each food item and relearn each process associated with shopping. Passing by a selection of apples, you would need to touch, smell, and taste each one to determine whether it was good to eat. You might notice the rolling baskets at the front of the store, wondering about their purpose as you juggled canned goods in your arms.

Thankfully, God created us in such a way that once we learn a concept, we have the ability to retain it by giving it a name. Once an item has a name, we can put it in a category and make generalizations. Knowledge structures organize memories and guide our behavior. We understand that every object, person, and situation, has its own unique characteristics. But we cannot escape from making generalizations. The ability to think begins with the ability to generalize and make assumptions. If we could not generalize, learning would be limited to discovery rather than to building on a foundation of what we have already discovered.

When I enter a grocery store and see a sign hanging from the rafters that says, "Produce," I predict that in that area of the store I am going to find a certain kind of food. Because I know the name "produce," I have an idea of what I will find if I head to that part of the store. Knowing the name "produce" allows me to make assumptions that guide my behavior. Under the "produce" category are the two major subcategories of "vegetables" and "fruit." Each of those subcategories contains more items. For example, I may find one bin of apples, or I may find an assortment of apples, each with its own name. If I find only rows of canned fruits and vegetables, I would be surprised for "produce" implies freshness.

The process of making generalizations from a name through categorization is similar for different items. Think of the word, "bicycle," and all of the related information we know just by knowing the categories it belongs to as well as the subcategories below it. From "transportation" to "touring bike" we can generalize up, down, and sideways as we communicate with others. The challenge comes when we move from concrete objects to abstract processes, ideas, or roles. Think of the word "wife." Though we can probably agree on what a "wife" is, if I ask several people to define the concept of a "good wife," I might get different answers.

Cognitive Schemata… the Stories in Our Minds

A complex web of concepts and categories are fashioned together in knowledge structures in our minds. A single structure, a schema, is linked with other schemata to form complex mental structures. Our schemata guide our social interaction by providing a framework for perceiving information, processing that information, and storing it in memory. We retrieve information from memory when our schemata are accessed by our senses or by new information.

When we wished to escape our village and have a weekend of rest, my husband and I traveled to a guesthouse in a neighboring city. After a relaxing shower, my thoughts often turned to my childhood, especially the lazy summer days spent visiting my grandparents. Eventually, I realized that the guesthouse workers dried their towels on a clothesline in the sun. My grandmother had also dried her towels on a clothesline. The roughness of the towels and the smell of sunshine were accessing childhood memories of more simple times when I visited my grandmother.

Schemata can be accessed by any of our senses. Understanding the power that smells have to evoke memories is a driving force behind the perfume industry. It is interesting to witness the schematic activation that occurs when friends get together and begin to tell stories. One may tell a story of a car wreck. That story reminds another of a tornado incident. Tornado stories are told for a while, and then someone tells a story of a bridge collapsing. Such episodes of one story activating another have led researchers to believe that perhaps our schemata are stored by large general categories in our memory systems (Howard, 1987). Researchers interested in schema theory continue to investigate the many unknowns of how we form, process, and store cognitive schemata. Clinical psychologists are even studying an organized treatment program referred to as schema therapy that counselors can use in addressing mental health issues (van Vreeswijk, Broersen, & Nadort, 2012).

One thing that has been discovered is that when we experience a recurring situation, such as riding in a bus, we tend to generalize the situation in memory. We usually forget the details of each particular situation. The more times we experience something, the less likely we are to recall each incident. From our experiences, our memories, a schema quickly emerges of that situation. We develop a "riding the bus" schema. This schema contains the concepts and categories we must understand in order to ride a bus such as "bus," "bus driver," "seat," etc. If asked, you could probably describe what it is like to ride a bus. If you have ridden a lot of buses in your life, you would have difficulty remembering each individual time you rode a bus. You may have a particular bus-riding memory, however, if something occurred during the experience that made it unusual.

A schema can be composed of steps or "slots" that describe a situation or process. These steps guide our behavior and make relearning a process unnecessary. Returning to the grocery store example, a grocery store schema contains multiple elements. It involves going someplace other than one's home, selecting an item or items that will eventually be eaten, paying for the item(s), and leaving the store with the item(s). A particular event of going to a grocery store changes depending upon how the different slots are filled. Since a grocery store schema has a slot for leaving the store with the items, the schema changes whether one has to box one's own groceries, there is a sacker and plastic bags are provided, or the customer is expected to provide reusable bags. In spite of all of the ways that a trip to the grocery store can differ, if a friend tells me she went to the grocery store, communication takes place because we both share a grocery store schema. I do not have to know the details of her visit. Having a schema, knowing the "story," of "going to the grocery store" allows us to communicate.

As grocery stores have enlarged their inventory to include selling ready-to-eat selections or items that are unrelated to food, such as toys, my grocery store schema has enlarged. Though grocery stores throughout the world may look different and sell different items, the grocery store schema is similar worldwide. Knowing the grocery store schema allows me to walk into a grocery store in the United States, China, or Kenya, and know what to expect. Whether the store is actually an open-air market, a neighborhood boutique, or a large discount warehouse, the schema remains similar.

When we experience something for the first time, new schemata are created, and learning occurs. The more times we experience the situation, the more generalized the schema becomes. Schemata can also be formed by hearing the story of another's experience or through fantasizing about a particular situation. The media are experts at creating or influencing our schemata. We may watch a commercial on television where we are thrust into someone else's story. We may hear messages that "normal" people act in a given manner. We witness others' fictionalized experiences and subconscious expectations are created within us. We find ourselves with schemata that influence what we expect to occur in a given situation, and we are left feeling that "something is missing" if our experience differs.

For example, what is your idea of the perfect Christmas? Perhaps you have heard someone say, "It just doesn't feel like Christmas this year." Our schemata help us determine what is "normal." Our Christmas experiences which began in childhood created schemata which contain certain emotional expectations. As stated earlier, schemata are formed not only by what we experience personally but by stories we hear or see. Expectations are created in us by others, such as the media. Our idea of the perfect Christmas may include snow and sleigh rides, even if we live in a desert and have never been in a sleigh.

Learning occurs not only when new schemata are created but also when our current schemata are altered. A schema may enlarge to include new experiences or change in some way, such as when we change our first impression of someone after spending time with him or her. Our schemata broaden to include new experiences such as when a familiar grocery store is remodeled, and we discover they've added an electronics section. Unless all of the grocery stores we enter also sell televisions, however, we will keep our grocery store schema but develop a "superstore" subschema.

It is truly mind-boggling when we consider all of the information we can access in a given schema. Using just one example, not only do we have a general "going to the grocery store" schema, we have numerous subschemata that cover the various types of stores. Remember the first time you entered a vast warehouse-type store? As you explored the aisles and amenities you were forming subschemata to attach to your superstore subschema to guide your behavior the next time you entered such a store. I once overheard my teenage daughter counseling her younger brother about how to approach a food sample cart while in such a store. "Just walk slowly by, looking in the other direction. Stop, and look at something, then casually turn your head toward the food cart..."

We develop new behavioral schemata for novel experiences, but we also constantly add to our knowledge by discovering new concepts. Imagine walking down a grocery store aisle. You pass by familiar items (concepts), grabbing what you need. If you see something you cannot identify, you stop. If the item is not too big, you may pick it up or touch it. If it is a fresh item, you may even smell it. You are using your senses to figure out where to place this item in the web of categories and schemata in your mind. You read the label, if there is one. You may even show the item to others you are with to get their opinions. You make a preliminary decision as to whether it is something you might like. If you decide to purchase the item to try it, you will continue to access schemata as you deal with the new item. Whether it is fresh, comes in a bottle, a can, or a box, you have a schema that will tell you how to deal with it. Once you have "experienced" the item, you can place it in its proper category of "things I buy regularly," "things I buy occasionally," or "things that I do not plan to purchase again."

Grocery store management is notorious for changing store layouts and moving items on the shelves. They know that when we are familiar with things, we rely on our schemata and are able to move quickly. We do not stop and pay attention in the same way we would if we were in a new environment. Changing a store layout will slow us down, make us concentrate on forming a new schema, and might even cause us to purchase an item we discover along the way.

One of the most important functions of schemata is to lessen our stress in new situations by providing guidelines for our behavior. A well-oiled schema is familiar and the familiarity makes us comfortable. Depending upon the importance we give to an event, changing a schema can make us physically and emotionally uncomfortable. While it might be easy to adjust our schemata when faced with changes in a grocery store, it can be a different matter when changes occur in something closer to our hearts, such as a beloved church. If some are used to holding hymnbooks during a worship service, for example, then the transition of keeping their hands by their sides and following the words on a projected screen may seem strange. Though they may understand the benefit of lifting their heads in song, it is possible that for some, their "singing during worship schema" has been reinforced through the years by an accompanying weight of something in their hands. For some, the lack of such a comforting weight when they sing may physically feel wrong because it is at odds with their schema. Their brains are telling them that something is missing. It may take a period of being uncomfortable before they develop a new schema that does not include holding a hymnbook. Those who have never held a hymnbook while singing, however, might feel equally awkward to have their hands bound by such a weight.

In the story at the beginning of the chapter, I stated that my wedding schema had let me down. I have observed many weddings in my life and experienced my own. My wedding schema includes concepts of a bride (usually in a fancy dress), a groom, someone officiating over the marriage ceremony, respectful witnesses, and an attitude of reverence. I have observed enough home weddings to know that not all weddings begin with a bridal entrance. Therefore, my wedding schema starts with the bride and groom standing together in front of witnesses and before the officiator. Next in my schema, the officiator conducts a ceremony which involves the bride and groom making vows to each other. Finally, the couple is pronounced husband and wife, and everyone celebrates. When our cultural informers in our village told us we were going to a wedding, my wedding schema kicked in. I dressed and eagerly walked downtown expecting to see certain things. My expectations were not met.

When we have a schema and expectations are not met, various emotions result. Depending upon the situation, those emotions could range from excitement and awe to confusion, fear, disappointment, or even anger. When we experience something totally unexpected, we have choices of how to react. We can admit that our schema was wrong, reject it, and create a new schema, or we can enlarge or adjust our current schema.

Totally rejecting a schema is very difficult. For example, if we have developed a schema that a friend is a "nice guy" and one day the friend screams at us, we usually do not say, "We were wrong. He is not a nice guy." We are more likely to try to come up with reasons for his unexpected behavior such as, "He must be having a bad day." Only after multiple repetitions of bad guy behavior will we question our original schema.

When our expectations are not met, we may also keep our old schema, perhaps enlarging or adjusting it somewhat, and create a separate subschema to cover the new experience. When I observed the Muslim wedding in our village, I did not say, "I was wrong about weddings. What I am witnessing now must be the true way a wedding is supposed to take place." I kept my wedding schema but realized I needed a new schema for a Muslim wedding. I did not create a schema to encompass all Muslim weddings from this one observation, however. I realized I needed more information before I could generalize. I asked our cultural informers as well as other Muslim friends about their wedding experiences. I learned that what I had witnessed was unique to our African village. The people called themselves Muslim but their wedding practices reflected their traditional religion. What I had witnessed was not indicative of Muslim weddings in other places. I therefore created a wedding schema that was unique for our village.

Since the interplay between creating, enlarging, and adjusting concepts and schemata occurs subconsciously as we go throughout our daily experiences, it is often our schemata that guide us rather than focused thought. Without asking for clarification, I might have made the mistake of reporting what I had witnessed as true of all Muslim weddings. I would have been wrong. We need to be careful and willing to stop, reflect, and separate expectations from truth. Otherwise, unexamined generalizations may lead to prejudice and error. The intricate web of concepts and schemata that form knowledge structures in our minds encourages us to generalize so that we can get on with our lives. As Christians, every day we are bombarded with messages that challenge biblical truth. Without conscious reflection and refutation, we can easily fall into error.

Many difficulties in relationships, especially marriages, occur because of differing schemata that create certain subconscious expectations. Each person brings to a relationship his/her own schemata that have been formed from personal past experiences, especially experiences from childhood. Such schemata guide expectations for daily life such as "the correct way" to celebrate birthdays, rear children, handle finances, clean the house, etc. Difficulties arise when those involved in a relationship are not aware of their expectations or do not communicate their expectations to others. Sharing childhood stories or talking about past experiences and reflecting on personal schemata may go a long way to resolving difficulties. In Part II we will discuss the effect that hearing stories about ourselves might have had on our personality development.

Cultural Schema Theory

Travel and living in a foreign country can be exhausting. Until we develop schemata that guide our interactions, we are constantly in a learning mode. Faced with new sights, smells, and concepts, life can quickly become overwhelming. We may find that we do not have schemata to cover our new circumstances. We try to fit what we experience into existing schemata. However, if the experience doesn't fit, we literally do not know how to behave until we form a schema. When we do not have a schema to tell us how to react, we are sure to experience emotions like awe, fear, or even anger. We may even begin to question our existing schemata. Once while teaching a newcomer the intricacies of driving in our country, I was startled that she ran a stop sign. When I pointed out the sign and the necessity of stopping, she remarked, "Oh, does that sign mean 'stop' in this country, too?"

As human beings, we develop schemata that reflect our culture. Here is a definition of cultural schemata that will serve as a review for what we have learned.

"Cultural schemas are generalized collections of the knowledge that we store in memory through experiences in our own culture. Cultural schemas contain general information about familiar situations and behavioral rules as well as information about ourselves and people around us. Cultural schemas also contain knowledge about facts we have been taught in school or strategies for problem solving, and emotional or affective experiences that are often found in our culture. These cultural schemas are linked together into related systems constructing a complex cognitive structure that underlies our behavior" (Nishida, 2005, p. 404).

One of the characteristics of an expert is the ability to categorize and notice variations that escape most of us. I walk by a garden and see flowers and plants. A gardener sees various types of flowers and plants, perhaps knowing their common names and categorizing them according to whether they are annuals or perennials. A botanist walking by the same garden sees much more and can probably identify and name the individual plant species, telling us not only about the individual plants but discussing the various parts (subcategories) of the plants. The botanist may even have more specialized knowledge, able to break down the plant parts all the way to their various types of cells.

Experts who study schema theory may spend their lives researching how we store information and how our minds work. Proponents of culture schema theory have identified at least eight types of cultural schemata that people may hold (Nishida, 2005). They include schemata about ourselves, others, and expected roles. They include schemata about items and events, contexts, and procedures. They include schemata that provide us with problem-solving strategies and schemata about attitudes and emotions. The content of each of these types of schemata differs according to our culture. The schemata form a web of knowledge in our minds as one schema accesses another.

For example, you realize you are thirsty. Your context schema kicks in and you notice your surroundings. Your context or situation determines your procedure for getting something to drink. If you are at home, you may reach for a glass and go to the water faucet or the refrigerator water filter. You may open the refrigerator for a soft drink. If you do not find your desired soft drink, you are faced with a problem and your problem solving schema is activated. This problem is different from the one you would encounter if you realized you were thirsty and you were riding on a bus in a foreign country and the next stop was hours away. Whereas the first situation might access a frustration emotion schema, the second situation might access stronger emotions if you realize it may be hours before you can quench your thirst. Imagine feeling thirsty, realizing you are in the context of your home, grabbing a glass and walking to the water faucet, only to realize you now live in a country in which you should not drink water that has not been filtered. Until you develop a schema where you automatically reach for filtered water, you will have to consciously pay attention to what you are doing whenever you feel thirst. If you wake up in the middle of the night and are thirsty, do not be surprised if you forget and drink unfiltered water from the faucet.

Adapting to a host culture means developing cultural schemata that work within that culture. Individuals who travel to live in another culture for a time are called sojourners because they intend to return to their home cultures someday. Immigrants are not sojourners because they usually do not intend to return to their home countries. International students, international aid workers, mission volunteers, and foreign diplomats are all considered sojourners.

It is natural to assume that others share the schemata that guide our everyday behavior. When sojourners enter a new culture, they often make the mistake of judging people's behavior based on the sojourner's own expectations. After all, one of the roles of our schemata is to tell us what "proper" behavior is. Unfortunately, what is proper in one culture may not be proper in another. Instead of relying on their cultural schemata, sojourners need to be willing to have new experiences and listen to stories about the host culture in order to develop cultural schemata pertinent to the host culture. Sojourners' new cultural schemata will not replace the schemata that guide behavior when in their home culture. The new cultural schemata will, however, allow the sojourner to be at ease and communicate more effectively while in the host culture. Unfortunately, instead of learning how people in their new culture experience life, I have seen too many sojourners cling to their cultural expectations and berate the locals for not doing things "properly."

While we live as sojourners in another culture, life becomes an adventure. Although we may share many general schemata with people from other cultures, our unique experiences have provided us with distinctive schemata. God placed us in our home cultures just as he placed others in their cultures. It is rare to find people who do not feel that their own culture is the best. As we sojourn in other cultures, we must not only develop new cultural schemata to help us behave appropriately, we must go further to understand assumptions about reality that people in our host culture may take for granted. If we have not already done so, we must also come to terms with the assumptions about reality that we take for granted.

The Influence of Worldview

Assumptions about the nature of the universe are embedded within each culture. These assumptions – our worldview – guide our interpretation of the world. Our worldview influences our values and what we believe to be important. There is evidence to show that our worldview can actually influence what we see. For example, research has shown that when individuals from societies that value group membership are asked to look at a picture, they tend to focus on the whole picture including details in the surrounding background (Nisbett, 2003). When individuals from societies that stress the individual are shown the same picture, they tend to pay attention to a prominent, isolated detail and ignore the background. What we value can color what we see.

Our worldviews may differ not only by whether we value group membership or individualism, but also by our concept of time. As U.S Americans, we tend to live in the future. Today is useful for how it can be used to impact the future. For others reared in more precarious circumstances, individuals may be more interested in the past and what occurs today. Our talk of future things may confuse them because they have difficulty with the concept of a positive future.

As sojourners, we may adapt to our host cultures by developing cultural schemata to help guide our behavior. We can learn to navigate a foreign grocery store or even learn what to expect at a wedding. Changing our assumptions about reality or changing others' assumptions is a different matter. It often takes the supernatural work of Christ to influence worldviews. This supernatural work must not only take place in the lives of the people with whom we are working, it must take place in us as well. Too often as a U.S. American, I have been guilty of assuming that all peoples see the world as I do. I gave my life to Christ at a young age and grew up in the church. As an adult, I have realized how much my biblical worldview has been impacted by my U.S. American worldview. I cannot help but interpret Scripture through my own cultural lens. Others cannot help but interpret Scripture through their lenses. That is the way God created us. As believers, however, we must allow the Bible to come alive, to allow Christ to develop His worldview, His truths, in us. Only then will a developing biblical worldview influence our existing worldview.

What is so powerful about stories? **Schemata are types of stories in our minds that hold our memories, help us understand our**

surroundings, and guide our behavior every day. We could not function without them. We develop a sense of community when we share positive experiences with others. The Bible is full of stories of how lives were changed when individuals encountered the living God. It is not enough to be able to recite the biblical stories, however. We must question the way we look at the world and allow our lives to be changed by biblical truth. When we consciously work to develop a biblical worldview, we are more likely to develop corresponding schemata that encourage us to behave like Christ. The first step is to slow down and reflect on why we behave as we do. Are we holding on to old schemata? How do our worldview assumptions influence us? Are we asking others to behave in a manner that reflects our cultural schemata or biblical truth? Do we even know the difference? Perhaps there are practices that we need to change in our lives. Perhaps we need to learn some new stories. It is all about the renewing of our minds…

Mark's language helper, Muhammed, arrived at the front door forty-five minutes late. Stacey had given up waiting and had gone into the kitchen to peel carrots for lunch. Mark had grabbed his Bible, but was too annoyed to read. When Muhammed finally arrived, grinning as if he had done nothing wrong, Mark grimaced. They would have to have a talk. Obviously, Muhammed did not understand the importance of time.

Resources:

Howard, R. W. (1987). *Concepts and schemata: An introduction.* Philadelphia, PA: Taylor and Francis.

Nisbett, R. E. (2003). *The geography of thought: How Asians and Westerners think differently...and why.* New York, NY: Free Press.

Nishida, H. (2005). Cultural schema theory. In W. B. Gudykunst (Ed.), *Theorizing about intercultural communication,* 401-418. Thousand Oaks, CA: Sage.

Van Vreeswijk, M., Broersen, J., & Nadort, M. (Eds.). (2012). *The Wiley-Blackwell handbook of schema therapy: Theory, research and practice (Wiley Clinical Psychology Handbooks, 1st ed.).* West Sussex, United Kingdom: John Wiley & Sons.

CHAPTER 2

Orality and Literacy

Muhammad looked at Mark and Stacey sitting next to each other on the couch. When he arrived, Mark was agitated and quickly thrust a notebook into his hands, telling him he already planned the language lesson, and they had better get started as they were late. Muhammad had not even been able to tell them about the new baby that arrived that morning. He stopped by the maternity ward to see his wife and peek at the baby snuggled against her breast. His mother-in-law and three of his wife's sisters encircled the bed. Surely these Americans would want to celebrate this new life with him, his first child. Since learning English at the university, Muhammad had often worked with outsiders wanting to learn His language. It was easy money. Foreigners paid too much, often agreeing to the first price he told them. Stacey kept looking toward the kitchen. Did they have children? Mark pointed to a picture of a car and asked Muhammad to write the word for car in the notebook. Muhammad complied. From the corner of his eye, in another room, he saw a baby playing in a crib enveloped in a mosquito net. Poor thing…to be all alone…

Individualism and Collectivism

I loved to watch my African neighbor make manioc couscous. First, she bought sacks of manioc which resembled large white yams. She peeled and grated them by hand, spreading the gratings out on plastic sheets in the sun to dry. When they were dry, she gathered the gratings up in baskets and took them to the mill to be ground into couscous. Then, using a special pot, she steamed the couscous until it was soft. The last step was packaging it in small plastic bags which she sold once a week in the downtown market on market day. The whole process took about three days. It did not take me long to add up all she was spending on such things as the manioc, grinding, firewood, and plastic bags. I did a cost-benefit ratio, and I did not like what I found. For the several days' work, she was actually losing money. I could not wait to share my findings with her. My assumption was that she prepared the manioc couscous because she wanted to make money. Why else would she work for three days if she did not hope to make a profit? I was wrong. When I shared my analysis, suggesting that she do something more profitable, she just stared at me. "But, this is what I do…" she said. She was one of several who had taken on the role of making manioc couscous for the community. Though I am sure she would have preferred to have made money, making money was not her objective. If she did not prepare the manioc couscous, who would? She gained satisfaction by fulfilling her role. I had approached the situation from my individualistic worldview whereas she was considering the same situation from a collectivistic worldview. We each shook our heads at the other's foolishness.

As we saw in the previous chapter, there are various ways of looking at the world around us. These cultural assumptions influence how we view ourselves, judge others, and even interpret Scripture. It is always risky to characterize cultures and people by lumping them together in one group. To do so inevitably causes comparisons between groups, such that one group is seen as "better" than the other. However, there is also the risk that if we do not categorize and point out differences, we tend to assume that others view the world in the same way we view it. Individualism and collectivism are two broad worldview categories that can help us better understand ourselves and others.

Societies that tend to be individualistic and those that tend to be collectivistic assume different things about the world. Individualistic societies assume people are independent of each other. Individualists value personal uniqueness and independence. Status is achieved through individual effort. They believe group boundaries are negotiable and group needs must be balanced with individual goals.

Collectivistic societies assume that groups bind individuals and obligate its members to each other. Collectivists value duty to the group and group harmony, especially when the lives of members of a group are intertwined such as in a family. Status is ascribed, in that one is born into particular groups. An important part of living is fulfilling roles and learning to make the most of whatever responsibilities or benefits those roles bring.

Researchers often disagree on what traits constitute individualism or collectivism. Depending upon what one measures, there is a certain degree of individualism and collectivism in all cultures. People's beliefs in their right to self-fulfillment, duty to their family, degree of competitiveness, and how much they value privacy are some of the traits that have been measured. Some people can be highly individualistic in one area but collectivistic in another. For example, researchers have found that Japanese tend to be more collectivistic than U.S. Americans when it comes to communication style, personal uniqueness, and view on privacy. However, when competitiveness is measured, there is little difference (Oyserman, Coon, & Kemmelmeier, 2002).

Whether one can be labeled individualistic or collectivistic comes down to a person's overall beliefs and behavior. Valuing personal success and self-fulfillment, creating and maintaining a positive self-image, and openly expressing one's opinions, are considered individualistic behaviors. Individualists tend to separate persons from their pasts or social contexts and believe that anyone can achieve whatever they work toward. For individualists, self-fulfillment is often considered a right even if in fulfilling personal desires others suffer. Proverbs such as, "The end justifies the means," or "You can't argue with success," or "The sky is the limit," encourage individualistic values.

In collectivism, a person's identity is bound with the group. Individuals are expected to expend personal effort and do their best because their best benefits group goals. When the group succeeds, then the person is seen as successful. Groups may consist of "in-groups" like family, extended family, and religious groups, or "out-groups" in which people come together for a limited time for a particular purpose. Collectivistic people tend to communicate indirectly and seek to avoid confrontation in order to maintain group harmony. Proverbs such as, "If people are of one heart, even yellow earth can become gold," or "The spectators see more of the game than the players," or "A friend to everybody is a friend to nobody" encourage collectivistic values.

U.S. Americans are considered the most individualistic people in the world, even more so than Europeans, leading some researchers to question whether grouping societies together and calling them "Western" is accurate (Oyserman et al., 2002). Though U.S. Americans value relationships, belong to groups, and may feel a duty to a group, we tend to join groups to fulfill personal desires. We, as individuals, choose which groups we will join. In the United States, we tend to explain our motives for joining a group. If it is not obvious that the group will benefit us personally, others might suspect our motives. Individuals are often considered as separate from their context, such as their "roots" or their family. We may even encourage individuals to separate from their family if it appears the family is hindering the individual's personal success.

Chinese society is considered the most collectivistic in the world. This does not mean that in Chinese society individual talents are not recognized. However, as one Chinese researcher put it, individual talents must be harnessed for the good of the group (Li, 2012). This researcher remarked that U.S. Americans often misunderstand Chinese classrooms, thinking that the strict discipline and emphasis on group harmony is stifling. She likened the classroom to an orchestra. Each student has gifts and strengths that must be brought under the control of the teacher/conductor so that beautiful music will result. When a student's ability has contributed to the group's outcome, that student experiences a feeling of accomplishment just as a violinist might feel at the end of a concert.

I thought of that analogy while listening to a local orchestra warm up before a performance. Each person onstage was doing his/her own thing. The resulting sound was a raucous mess. However, when the conductor gained the stage and lifted his baton, all was still. As one, the various musicians contributed to the performance. I suppose it could be said that they were no longer free. The musicians were restricted by the music in front of them and the conductor's hand. They were all smiling when the performance was over, however, as was the audience. Though this is a simplistic analogy, for the beauty of the music changes with who controls the group, it gave me a better understanding of collectivism.

In the late 1800s, a British anthropologist, Sir Edward Tylor, popularized the idea that cultures evolve. In this idea, which came to be labeled "social Darwinism" by those who disagreed, cultures begin by being primitive and child-like but eventually evolve into individualistic, Western-type cultures. Though anthropologists have since chronicled how so-called "primitive" cultures are actually very complex, the idea that cultures evolve and that individualism is associated with modernism remains in popular thought.

In our rhetoric, we often talk of "developing" nations. Though there is no single understanding of what makes one nation "developed" and another "developing," there is a tendency to link "developed" with industrialized. Nations are categorized by their rates of life expectancy, schooling, and level of income. Those that have higher rates are considered more developed. In this rating, there is an inherent, almost unquestioned belief that higher life expectancy, level of schooling, and level of income equals a better existence. Global organizations such as the

United Nations Educational, Scientific, and Cultural Organization (UNESCO) generally follow these beliefs.

Some have questioned whether these economic variables such as a higher life expectancy actually equal a better quality of life. Living longer may mean living longer while incapacitated. Some have suggested that rating countries according to quality of life would be more useful. However, because of differing beliefs about what constitutes "quality of life" such a rating would be difficult. Certainly, those with individualistic tendencies and those with collectivistic tendencies would disagree about how such a concept should be measured.

What causes some cultures to value individualism and others to value collectivism? One researcher traced individualism to early Greek thought and collectivism to more holistic Chinese thought (Nisbett, 2003). Others have associated individualism with early hunting societies and collectivism with farming societies (Hofstede, 1980). Some have noted that people tend to be more collectivistic when they experience a lot of social upheaval (Maranz, 2001). In those situations, people need to band together to share resources.

It has been found that literacy can lead to individualistic behavior, though there are highly literate collectivistic cultures as well. Much depends upon which values literacy upholds. However, the act of reading and writing allows one to separate from the group, be alone, and gain knowledge from a text. Those who cannot read or write must depend upon others to teach them orally. In the next section, we will look at literacy and how the ability to read and write might affect culture.

Literacy and Illiteracy

Though literacy is defined in different ways, all definitions include an ability to read and write. More and more, the definition of literacy has come to include abilities one learns through schooling. After a meeting of literacy experts, the United Nations Educational, Scientific, and Cultural Organization (UNESCO) offered this definition:

> Literacy is the ability to identify, understand, interpret, create,
> communicate and compute, using printed and written
> materials associated with varying contexts. Literacy involves a
> continuum of learning in enabling individuals to achieve his or
> her goals, develop his or her knowledge and potential, and
> participate fully in community and wider society
> (UNESCO, 2005, p. 21).

The fact that UNESCO included in its definition a reference to literacy as "enabling individuals to achieve his or her goals," illustrates how much global organizations are influenced by individualism.

Many people use the term "illiterate" to describe those who do not read or write. Using this term is problematic for several reasons. First, "illiterate" is defined differently by various countries. The Republic of Mali, for example, defines an illiterate as one who has never been to school. If adults there have never been to school but have learned to read and write, they are still considered illiterate. Some countries attach a level of schooling, be it first, second, or seventh grade, that one must attain to no longer be considered illiterate. Second, the prefix "il" is often attached to negate a word that is considered the accepted standard. Legitimate is positive whereas illegitimate is not. Legal is positive whereas illegal is not. Legible is positive whereas illegible is not. By using the term "illiterate," literacy becomes the approved standard and those who cannot read or write are considered incomplete or missing something. Third, using the term "illiterate" does not give credit for people's proficiency in orality, in the vast oral tradition in which people have been communicating and which has served various cultures well for thousands of years.

UNESCO publications have acknowledged that the term "illiterate" is increasingly unacceptable. Often, illiterates are seen as those who are on the fringes of modernity, those who have been left behind and have difficulty understanding modern life. In our rhetoric, often illiteracy has been likened to a disease, as publications talk about eradicating it or wiping it out in a given time period. In attempting to encourage people to become literate, some have emphasized illiteracy as being a negative state. One researcher in India asked a group of women who were standing outside in a public place to describe an illiterate woman. They said, among other things, that illiterate women are exploited, do not clean, and are ignorant. An illiterate woman nearby heard the remarks and was insulted, remarking that literates are always pushing cleanliness but do not consider the cost of soap and water (Chopra, 2004).

Many have adopted the term "oral communicator" to refer to those who prefer to process information orally rather than through literacy (Lausanne Committee for World Evangelization, 2005). Those who cannot read or write are automatically oral communicators. Because this term is used to identify how people process information, it is possible that someone can be literate and also an oral communicator. Understanding whether people prefer to gain knowledge and process information from texts or orally from other people is important when deciding how one will share information with them.

Because those in the academic community define themselves and others through literacy, referring to someone as an oral communicator can be problematic. Many who are highly literate consider themselves to be oral communicators also just because they speak. But they may not understand the distinct communication characteristics of oral cultures. Without an understanding of orality, many do not understand that once literate, one's oral communication often changes also.

When writing for the general population of Americans who may be unfamiliar with orality, I use the term, "nonliterate." Though this term also describes a person in relation to literacy, it is not as judgmental as "illiterate." A nonliterate adult is therefore an adult who cannot receive information by reading and who does not communicate with others through writing (Thompson, 2014). All nonliterate adults are oral communicators.

It is estimated that a minimum of 750 million adults in the world today are nonliterate. Some of those live as a minority in individualistic or collectivistic cultures where the majority of the population is literate.

The literate majority may not be aware of the nonliterates among them. Such is the case in the United States, even though it is estimated that at least seven million English-speaking adults living in the United States are totally nonliterate and another 30 million have only very basic literacy skills. That amounts to at least 30 million people who would have difficulty participating in our typical churches because they cannot read the monthly newsletter, Sunday School literature, bulletin, hymn books, nor follow the projected words on a screen during worship services. More significantly, they cannot read the Bible for themselves.

Some people are nonliterate because they speak a language that has never been written. A language is considered living if it is the mother tongue of at least one person. It is thought that only half of the estimated 7,105 living languages today have a developed writing system.

Some adults are nonliterate because they grew up in an oral culture where oral tradition was the norm. Literacy is tied to the government and schools, which may or may not be seen favorably. In Nigeria, for example, non-Arabic literacy and schools were introduced by the British colonizers. When required to send their children to school, traditional nobles sometimes sent their slaves instead, not wanting their own children to be influenced by a foreign government. Across much of the world today, oral cultures and oral tradition is still the norm.

Oral Cultures

Traditionally, oral cultures have been considered as those societies that are untouched by writing. In today's world, anyone who purchases a manufactured product or fills a prescription is immediately confronted by the written word. Yet, there are cultures where the majority of the people are oral communicators and are comfortable processing information orally. Thus, an oral culture is one that values oral communication, oral tradition, and where adults teach or pass along their culture using oral instructional strategies.

Though oral communication is the primary form of human communication in literate cultures as well as oral cultures, oral communication in literate cultures often begins with a text. Speech writing may be an oxymoron, but it is a respected profession. Plays begin with a script. Songs must be published to be owned. Music is written. Poetry is quoted from a memorized text.

People in oral cultures do not have the option of beginning with a text. To do so would probably be seen as confining and boring compared to the rich tradition of oral art. Literates in individualistic cultures learn to speak as they write, to-the-point, directly, and sometimes in a confrontational manner. In oral cultures, sound is everything. Flowery language and ancient rhetorical traditions are prized. Children speak directly. The mark of an adult is one who peppers his/her speech with proverbs, similes, stories, and formulaic sayings. Adult speech is usually indirect, sometimes obtuse.

Oral cultures are by their nature collectivistic. In many such cultures, the concept of solitude or being alone is equated with evil. Infants are almost always with their mothers or other female family members. They grow up in a holistic, adult world, understanding more and more of what goes on around them as they develop. Early in my ministry, I tried to separate mothers and children during Bible studies because that is what I was used to. Babies will distract mothers, and if we want the mothers to be able to concentrate, I believed we should separate them from their babies. Then I learned that in many oral cultures, unless a secret ritual is occurring, children are usually expected to be present if something is worthwhile. To exclude them is to imply that the teaching is not that important. It is believed that they will grasp whatever they can and that whatever is beyond their capabilities of understanding will simply pass over their heads. Babies will distract mothers. That is what babies do. Trying to orchestrate events so that distractions are minimized is actually more distracting than dealing with the distractions as they occur naturally.

The concept does not exist in oral cultures that one must be specially trained or certified before one is qualified to teach younger children. Practical knowledge is usually shared freely for the good of the community. Generally, once someone knows something or has learned a general skill, he/she is expected to pass it along to someone younger who needs to know it. Children learn through observation and imitation, usually without explanation. A lot of time is spent helping children learn to identify and name objects in the natural world around them. They grow up surrounded by people who are ready to teach them. The proverb, "It takes a village to raise a child" summarizes the attitude.

Specialized knowledge is divided and shared among the community. Those with special skills are expected to practice them for the good of the community as each one depends upon the other. Whether it be recognizing plants for their healing properties, knowing how to navigate by the stars, understanding how to set a broken bone, or something as simple as making manioc couscous on market day, each one has a responsibility and an identity.

In some oral cultures, certain specialized knowledge is passed from generation to generation through rote memorization. Without written records, some question whether what has been passed along is actually verbatim. However, one anthropologist who transcribed the words to a ritual that one man was teaching another returned after nine years to find the same man repeating the words exactly. In some cultures, only certain groups are allowed to share memorized historical stories and only certain people are allowed to hear them.

People in oral cultures engage in informal learning as well as formal learning. What differentiates informal learning from formal learning is that informal learning is usually practical and occurs in the context of daily life with family or peers as teachers. Formal learning often involves specialized knowledge and is out of the ordinary. It can be institutionalized as in schooling.

Nonliterate schools are held for a particular purpose such as to lead an age-group through initiation into adulthood or to teach divination or sorcery. In such cases, students are removed from their homes for a given amount of time and learn from those who are in authority over them. Even in schools in oral cultures, students must usually pass exams before they are considered "graduates." The exams are not written tests but oral exams in which the student must successfully answer questions or exhibit their knowledge or a learned skill.

Formal learning does not have to be institutionalized as in a school. Events where there is a demonstration of oral art in that a "performer" chants epic poems or narratives to entertain or pass along history are also examples of formal learning in that they are out of the ordinary. Apprenticeships in which parents make a formal agreement with a specialist to apprentice their child is another example of formal learning. In such cases, the child often lives with the "master," perhaps beginning by sweeping the work area or running errands. Eventually, as he/she is able, the child takes on more responsibility.

In oral cultures, daily life is all about sound and word play. Riddles, name-calling, jokes, proverbs, formulaic sayings, greetings, goodbyes, stories, specialized or secret language, and songs, for example, are not only necessary for memory, they make life interesting. People do not get "lost in a book," they get lost in each other. Gossip is a favorite past-time. When I was learning my African language, I often took a stool and sat with a group of women who gathered in the afternoon under a mango tree and braided each other's hair. As they spoke, I would sit with bowed head, listening to the rhythm of the language. Soon, I was able to recognize isolated words. I would lift my head and repeat the word. They would laugh and pat me on the head, proud of my efforts. I progressed from single words to phrases to sentences. When I could actually understand their conversation, it dawned on me that the gathering was an occasion for discussing in minute detail everyone and everything that happened on our street. It was a great language experience, but probably not the best place for a preacher's wife.

Researchers have shown that some of the differences between literates and nonliterates thought to be the result of learning to read and write were actually the result of going to school and learning a different communication style (Cole, 2005). For example, is it possible that women who have gone to school have an easier time negotiating government medical clinics? When going to health clinics, schooled women communicate orally just like nonliterate women. However, the schooled women are more likely to know how to speak directly with the medical workers, describing their symptoms or those of their children. On the other hand, even though women who have not been to school also communicate orally with clinic personnel, medical workers may lose patience with the nonliterate women when they speak indirectly about their concerns.

Stories

Storytelling in all cultures is as much a part of informal learning as formal learning. Fables teach cultural values. You may have grown up listening to the story of the little red hen who would not let the other animals eat the bread she had prepared because they refused to help in its preparation. This story of the little red hen teaches individualistic values.

Jerome Bruner, an American psychologist, believes that every culture needs stories to explain the out of the ordinary, those things that occur that challenge a schema. For example, a little girl attends a birthday party but does not eat the cake. In our birthday party schema, children normally eat cake. If a little girl attends a birthday party and is not eating cake, we want to know the reason. After hearing the story, we can decide what to do further. If her story is that she has an allergy to wheat, we react one way. If her story is that she saw the family dog licking the cake before it was served, we may react in a different way. No matter what her story, for the next birthday party we experience, we still retain our schema of children eating cake.

Stories have the advantage of making a point without being confrontational. That is one of the reasons they are so popular in collectivistic cultures. A writer discussing Native American parenting styles mentioned that parents often tell stories to their children as a way of commenting on a situation that concerns the child. I have found that storytelling is also an effective parenting method for use with teenagers. A few days before my son got his driver's license, I told the story I had heard of a boy who got his license in the morning and, eager to express his newfound freedom, went for a drive by himself in the afternoon and pulled out in front of a truck. The boy died in the accident. Following the story, my son looked at me and said, "Don't worry, Mother. I'll be careful." I had made my point.

As literates, many of our stories come from texts which have a linear plot line. Literates tend to like stories with a beginning, a middle, and an end. How a story ends often depends upon cultural expectations. U.S. Americans like happy endings. In some cultures, stories have no resolution, and in other cultures, such as French culture, the endings are often tragic. Because our stories are influenced by our cultural schemata, we tend to gloss over what does not fit with our worldview. How many times have we told the story of Joseph in prison, not emphasizing the years and years he endured before it was time for God to use him? Do we think of Ruth and Boaz hand in hand, walking off into the sunset holding little Obed? When I started memorizing Bible stories, I was surprised to learn what was and was not actually written in the story. Thankfully, we can go to the Book to check the text. For literates, learning a story includes checking the details frequently against a text.

Nonliterates, however, have no text with which to check their story. Some of the epic oral poetry have thousands of stanzas. How do the oral artists remember it all? That question led to the modern inquiry into orality. It was found that oral artists have a large storehouse of phrases which they repeat, phrases they can combine with others as they choose. There are about 25,000 repeated phrases in the 28,000 lines of Homer's oral poetry. Repetition, which literates may find boring, is a necessary part of learning in oral cultures. Oral artists, who often mix music, poetry, and stories in their renditions, may need some time after hearing a new story before they repeat it. They need to allow the new story to "sink in," to become a part of them. Then they can do what literates may have difficulty doing, which is to repeat a story after hearing it only once. The bards do not necessarily follow a linear progression in their storytelling but often thrust their audience into the middle of the action, adding details as they become necessary. The audience is not viewing a performance, but is expected to participate, to enter into the event, to respond with a repeated phrase or somehow show that they are engaged.

Secondary Orality

Are your favorite quotes from books or movies? More than thirty years ago, Walter Ong in his book *Orality and Literacy*, identified secondary orality as what occurs when literate people prefer to communicate orally through technology. Videos, movies, radio, and communicating orally through the Internet, are all oral communication methods that are based in literacy. In today's world, many literates using these strategies prefer not to communicate through reading or writing but choose to communicate orally. How many times do you pick up the phone instead of responding to someone's question through a letter or even email? Secondary orality is not the same as the orality of nonliterates in oral cultures, even though nonliterates in oral cultures also love television, radio, and movies. As mentioned previously, oral cultures are by definition collectivistic. Secondary orality, however, can thrive in individualistic cultures where community is often virtual. Individuals can remain anonymous, even re-fashion themselves according to whichever online group they join. They can choose to chat through writing or verbally but technology allows them to be present and not present at the same time.

Technology and digital cultures are also affecting literacy. As options for reading include more than the printed page, researchers are currently investigating the difference in retention between reading a story from a screen and reading it from a printed page (Mangen, Walgermo, & Bronnick, 2013). They are also looking into how searching the Internet affects cognitive reading processes when one wants to read a book. Preliminary reports show that there is a difference in how one's brain reacts when one is reading print or on a screen (Jabr, 2013).

As more and more church leadership is understanding the consequences of secondary orality for the church, there has been a growing interest in the topic. Trainings and resources are available to help churches learn more about the orality in their midst.

Navigating Oral Cultures

Since you are reading this text, I am assuming you are literate. Because oral strategies are based on the vagaries of sound, speaking in oral cultures is considered an art. Becoming proficient in orality will not be easy, especially if you are from an individualistic culture. Literates can find oral strategies effusive, flowery, and time-consuming. Those who are not used to speaking through a translator sometimes question if their words are being translated correctly. While speaking directly in English may not take long, communicating an idea in an oral culture can take considerable time. Used to depending upon a text, even when we speak, we often have difficulty understanding the importance of repetition or painting pictures with words.

Two young men who volunteered to spend several years beginning work in a village outside of the city where we lived were quick to learn the local language. They began using Bible stories to evangelize the people, and some were converted within a year. A local African pastor was invited to visit and teach the people. He began his teaching with a flowery prayer that seemed interminable to the young U.S. American men. "I couldn't believe it," one told me. "There was such a difference in the people. They came alive. They had listened to our simple prayers and understood. When the pastor prayed, however, it was obvious he had transported them to the throne of God."

Engaging in oral art comes after mastering the language. If you are working in a language that is not your mother tongue, you may have set your language learning goal too low. For many of us, we just want to learn enough to communicate as we understand communication in our culture. When my husband and I moved to an isolated village in West Africa, we already spoke the African language used there. Though there were some differences, we found that people did not have difficulty understanding us. However, we had a very difficult time understanding them. After mastering how to say something while sitting in a courtyard in one part of the village, I would try out what I had learned in another part of the village. There, the women would tell me I was saying whatever it was incorrectly. My husband had the same issue. We were very frustrated. It took about six months before we discovered the problem. Our village was divided into ten neighborhoods. Each neighborhood was known for a particular quality, such as the residents being hard workers, powerful sorcerers, lazy, friendly, or healers. The people in each neighborhood had tweaked the common language to make it their own. One who was born in that village would recognize which neighborhood a person was from after hearing a few sentences. No wonder we were having difficulty. To make matters worse, parents would appropriate a different neighborhood's style of language when speaking to their children if they wanted to make a point without being confrontational. For example, if a child from the industrious neighborhood was reluctant to work, the parent would switch and begin speaking to the child in the language of the lazy neighborhood. The child got the message. My husband and I decided that we would keep trying to learn the distinctions, but we could not wait to share Bible stories until we understood everyone. Since all of the people understood the language we spoke that mimicked those from a town several hours away, we spoke in that language and realized that we would probably have to ask those speaking to us to repeat themselves several times before we understood them.

Engaging in oral art and painting pictures with words requires a facility that few non-native speakers reach. However, that does not mean we cannot be effective in sharing the gospel. Being aware of orality and appreciating oral instructional strategies is the first step. In Part III, I will address ways in which you can increase your proficiency in oral cultures. Even during language study, there are some oral skills you can begin to develop that will help you communicate in oral cultures.

In the next chapter, we will consider differences in communication styles between individualistic and collectivistic cultures.

As the lesson grew to a close, Muhammad stood up. "Will you be able to be on time tomorrow?" Mark asked. Muhammad smiled.

"I am sorry I was late," he said. "My first child was born this morning, a daughter. I did not get much sleep last night."

"Congratulations!" Mark said heartedly as he shook his hand. "I understand how you must feel." He looked toward the bedroom. "Our son was born four months ago."

"May I visit your wife?" Stacey asked.

"She would love that!" Muhammad replied. "She doesn't speak English. But tomorrow, I can teach you the blessings one normally gives to a new baby, and you can practice them when you see her."

"That would be great," Stacey said. As Muhammad walked along the path to the maternity clinic, he thought of the two Americans. They were babies, just like his daughter. He would have to be patient.

Resources:

Chopra, P. (2004). Distorted mirrors: (de)centring images of the 'illiterate Indian village woman' through ethnographic research narratives. In A. Robinson-Pant (Ed.), *Women, literacy, and development* (pp. 35-56). New York, NY: Routledge.

Cole, M. (2005). Cross-cultural and historical perspectives on the developmental consequences of education. *Human Development, 48,* 195-216. doi: 10.1159/000086855

Hofstede, G. (1980). *Culture's consequences: International differences in work-related values.* Beverly Hills, CA: Sage.

Jabr, F. (2013). Why the brain prefers paper. *Scientific American, 309,* 48-53.

Li, J. (2012). *Cultural foundations of learning: East and West.* New York, NY: Cambridge University Press.

Mangen, A., Walgermo, B. R., & Bronnick, K. (2013). Reading linear texts on paper versus computer screen: Effects on reading comprehension. *International Journal of Educational Research, 58,* 61-68.

Maranz, D. (2001). *African friends and money matters.* Dallas, TX: SIL International.

Oyserman, D., Coon, H. M., & Kemmelmeier, M. (2002). Rethinking individualism and collectivism: Evaluation of theoretical assumptions and meta-analyses. *Psychological Bulletin, 128,* 3-72. doi: 10.1037//0033-2909.128.1.3

Thompson, L. W. (2014, November). *Teaching nonliterate adults: Insights from Illeris's learning theory.* Paper presented at the Commission for International Adult Education International Pre Conference (CIAE) to the 63rd American Association for Adult and Continuing Education (AAACE) Annual Conference, Charleston, SC. Available from ERIC.

United Nations Educational, Scientific, and Cultural Organization (UNESCO). (2005a). *Aspect of literacy assessment. Topics and issues from the UNESCO expert meeting,* June, 2003. Paris, France: UNESCO. Available from http://unesdoc.unesco.org/images/0014/001401/140125eo.pdf

CHAPTER 3

Intercultural Communication

Mark could not believe they had been living in the village for four months. He enjoyed his time with Muhammad as they walked the village paths in the early evening. Muhammad had suggested that instead of spending several hours studying flashcards that Mark should get out into the community and practice what they had discussed that morning. It had been difficult at first, but Mark knew that Muhammad was right. They often stopped by Muhammad's cousin's store. There, men from the village gathered in the early evening to play cards or talk about the day. When Mark and Muhammad arrived, the older men would shoo a youth from the wooden bench outside the store and motion to Mark to sit down. At first he refused, but Muhammad had told him to refuse is rude, so he squeezed himself into whatever space he was given. Sometimes the men talked or gestured or laughed uproariously. Mark couldn't get over the impression that they were usually laughing about him. Muhammad had told him that the Americans in their midst were the source of much village entertainment. Mark had learned to nod and smile. It didn't take long for him to exhaust his limited vocabulary. Sometimes he would daydream of the time when he would be able to preach in the local language, standing before the men as he had done at his church back in North Carolina...

Have you ever been speaking with someone and wished they would just get to the point? If so, it is possible that you were experiencing a clash of communication styles. The person speaking to you may have been frustrated because he/she had given you ample opportunity to pick up on his/her nonverbal symbols, but you obtusely refused to say what the person expected. In the first chapter, we looked at cultural schema theory and how cultural schemata influence our behavior depending upon our context. In this section, we will look at how our cultural schemata influence our face-to-face interaction with people from different cultures.

Intercultural Communication: Perception

We perceive what is going on in our surroundings through our senses. The first stage of perception is deciding what we will pay attention to. There is too much going on in our world for us to pay attention to everything. When I was a young mother, I learned to function with three preschoolers. I recognized which cries were serious, though most times it was their silence that prompted me to investigate. Now, with that time far behind me, I am sometimes in awe at how young mothers can continue to carry on a conversation while their toddlers are running every which way. I cannot help but follow the children with my eyes while the mother hardly looks in their direction. In order to carry on a conversation, the mothers have learned to block out distractions.

Do you know why health experts advise us not to go grocery shopping when we are hungry? It is because hunger is a basic human need. When we need something, we are more likely to pay attention to things in our environment that will meet that need. Surrounded by food in the grocery store, it is as if the food calls out to us. Even if we went into the grocery store planning to buy only a few items, we can find ourselves loading the cart.

Our cultural schemata influence what we see, do, and what we hear. My husband was reared in the country while I have lived in the city all my life. When we were dating and planned our first trip to see his parents on the farm, he assured me that I would sleep wonderfully because country nights were so peaceful, unlike the constant city noise that often awakened him. That first night at the farm, I could hardly sleep for the croaking of the frogs, the mooing of the cows, and the barking of the dogs. The next morning, he met me at breakfast, exclaiming how finally, he had had a peaceful night's sleep! He had not been kept awake as I had been because he had learned not to pay attention to country sounds and had not been bothered by them.

If we were born into an English-speaking household, we learned to pay attention to English sounds. Because vowel length may signal a regional accent but does not influence word meaning, English-speakers can generally understand someone whether they say "cat" or "caaaat," as Southerners are apt to do. Children born into other cultures where vowel length is connected to meaning must learn to pay attention to vowel length, or they will misunderstand those around them. In Japanese, for example, the only difference between the word for "aunt" and the word for "grandmother" is the length of a vowel.

Having paid attention to the particular sounds in a language all our lives, it is difficult to hear distinctions in another language that a native speaker can hear immediately. English speakers typically have difficulty with other languages that stress pitch or accent. Though having difficulty learning another language may lead us to think that other languages are more difficult compared to ours, children the world over learn language at about the same rate. Much of our language learning success is linked to how willing we are to enter another culture as a child.

Once we have decided to what we will pay attention in our environment, the second step in perception is organization. It is through our language that our perceptions are organized and characterized. At one time, it was thought that our language actually controlled what we could see. For example, different cultures group colors differently. It was thought that perhaps if a language did not have a color for "teal" for example, then perhaps the people who spoke that language could not recognize that color. It is now known that even if our language does not have a particular word for a color, the color can still be perceived, though some specialists, such as interior decorators, may be better at perceiving color differences than others.

Understanding a language can give tremendous insight into the culture that speaks that language. In the African language we learned, for example, the words for "woman" and "wife" were the same, just as the words for "man" and "husband" were the same. In that culture, it was expected that everyone would someday marry. Whereas in English, there is a generic word for "sister," in our African language, there were separate words for younger sister and older sister. If one wished to say, "This is my sister," one had to designate whether the sister was younger or older. Since information about family hierarchy is automatically given in introductions, we understood that family hierarchy is valued in that culture.

The third step in perception is interpretation, attaching meaning to what has been perceived. Depending upon our cultural schemata and the meaning we attach to certain things, people from different cultures may react to the same item or situation differently. Once while showing a picture book to a group of African children, I spied a picture of a large frog. "Do you eat frog legs?" I asked. They were horrified and loudly exclaimed their disgust. I turned the page where there was a picture of a big rat. "Do you eat rat?" they asked me excitedly. I was horrified and loudly exclaimed my disgust, much to their delight and protest that I was missing out on a delicacy.

Intercultural Communication: High Context or Low Context?

All communication takes place within a context that adds meaning to the communication (Gudykunst, 2005; Jandt, 2004; Tian, 2010). Though the words may be the same, someone hanging from a cliff who says, "Help me" is in a different situation than someone who is doing dishes at the sink and says, "Help me." The reaction to the same command will likely be different.

For some cultures, the context is actually part of the communication. Not only the persons involved in the communication but the situation and place work together to determine how the message is composed, sent, and received. These cultures are known as high-context cultures. In high-context cultures, communication is often indirect as figuring out the message from contextual clues is an important part of communication. Not surprisingly, high-context, indirect communication is usually found in collectivistic cultures. The messenger's needs or desires that he/she wants to present are not automatically found in the message alone.

In some oral cultures, society is such high-context that the actual language changes depending upon the context. Greetings may change depending upon the time of day, where one is, and whom one is greeting. As in the example of our village, language may change depending upon the place the conversation takes place. Languages such as these which have been turned into a form of oral art may be especially difficult for English speakers to learn unless they learn them in context.

In low-context cultures, the message is the most important part of the communication process. Low-context, direct communication is usually found in individualistic cultures. In these cultures, a lot of time is spent in preparing and presenting the message. The worth of the message is intrinsic in the message itself. Whereas in indirect communication the worth of the message is usually validated by the messenger, in direct communication, the message is often seen as standing alone. For example, some believe that people's character is not necessarily tied to how well they perform a job. In scandals regarding the U. S. presidency, many have stated that a president's private actions should not impact his job as president. In a high-context culture, however, the messenger's background and character and the worth of the message are often intertwined.

The United States is considered a low-context culture, though there are situations in which communication is high-context. For example, among family or friends who have known each other a long time and have shared life's stories, fewer words may be needed to communicate. A friend and I can finish each other's sentences. As a result, we often speak in half sentences not needing to complete a thought because we understand each other. It frustrates those around us, especially our children, because they have difficulty following our conversation. However, she and I communicate perfectly.

Often, couples in low-context cultures who have been together a long time use high-context communication. When a couple is sitting together watching television, and the wife says, "I'm cold," one would not expect the husband to ask her about her physical state. For many, normal behavior would be for the husband to get up and adjust the thermostat or get his wife a blanket. Of course, sometimes we can get the message wrong. Wives who use indirect, high-context communication often misinterpret low-context messages from their husbands. Sometimes when my husband comes into the house after working outside and announces, "I'm hungry," I understand his declaration to be a request that I fix him something to eat. If I am in the middle of a project, I may become frustrated, wondering why he cannot fix something himself instead of asking me to fix him something to eat when he knows I am busy. With time, I have learned that he may just be announcing his hunger and does not expect me to do anything. I have learned to ask for clarification instead of assuming I know what he is trying to communicate. In the same vein, sometimes wives will vent their frustration or talk about a certain situation that is puzzling them. Often, the husband is wondering how to respond, what his wife is wanting him to do about the situation when all she wants is someone to listen. I have learned to say, "I don't want you to do anything about this. I just need to share my thoughts." In saying that, my husband can relax and listen.

Even in low-context cultures, there are certain situations where people expect high-context communication to take place. Some people alter their language when speaking in a particular place, such as a church. Others use different language when they are speaking to their friends or to people whose positions, such as a judge, normally require respect. Understanding high-context communication situations such as these which occur within a low-context culture, can help us understand cultures where almost everyone, even strangers, use high-context communication almost exclusively. In communicating with strangers in a high-context culture, one must understand what restrictions the context, such as one's role or a place, may put on the communication.

Silence for many in low-context cultures may simply be something waiting to be filled. In high-context cultures, silence can hold as much meaning as speaking. Depending upon the context, silence may mean agreement. It can also mean disagreement.

For those of us unused to indirect communication, when we are engaged in intercultural communication, talking indirectly and using intermediaries instead of speaking directly or confronting the issue can seem like a waste of time. We may not understand how speaking directly can cause problems. When we are tempted to speak directly to someone in a high-context culture, we need to think of what might happen if we told our spouse, "Don't wear that. It makes you look fat."

Transmission Communication or Transaction Communication?

Closely tied with the setting of communication is the purpose of communication. Low-context, direct communication cultures often engage in transmission communication (Jandt, 2004). They believe that the purpose of communication is to transmit ideas. In this model, the source has a message he/she wants to share with a receiver or receivers. The messenger chooses how, when, and where the message will be shared. The message is shared through a "channel" which can be affected by "noise" or elements outside of the messenger's control. The receiver has to decode the message and may respond. How well one communicated can be measured by the receiver's reaction or understanding of the message.

In the transaction model of communication, which is usually seen in collectivistic cultures, the relationship between the messenger and the receiver are part of the message. The same words can be spoken to different people with different meanings. The messenger takes advantage of shared stories to aid in communication. In this model, respecting the relationship is sometimes considered to be more important than the words that are shared.

In our culture, we often see the transaction model of communication used with young people, the elderly, or those who are sick. Meeting a nursing home resident for the first time, we may take his/her hand and ask, "How are you?" We do not necessarily want a detailed response to our question. By expressing those words, however, we are acknowledging the hearer as a person.

Just as there is some individualism and some collectivism in every culture, there is some measure of direct and indirect communication as well as transmission and transaction communication in all cultures. Some of those who study communication argue that all effective communication is a transaction. People differ in their personalities and are influenced by the stories that define them. Some speak more directly while others speak indirectly. Those who grow up in a particular culture learn the communication "rules" without thinking of them. I have known Northerners who wonder why Southerners tend to ask personal questions. I have known Southerners who have shaken their heads at the apparent reserve of Northerners.

Effective intercultural communication involves understanding that communication often involves more than the simple transmission of ideas. In the next section, we will discuss some ways to increase our intercultural communication competence.

Effective Intercultural Communication

Understand that communication styles differ. Many times when entering a new culture, we are more worried about learning the language than learning to communicate. We may think if we can just use their language to transmit our ideas, then communication will take place. If only it were that easy.

There is not one "right" way to communicate something. Because culture and communication beliefs and methods are intertwined, understanding the culture will help us be better communicators in that culture. Even if we are beginning language study and may be frustrated because we cannot express our ideas, in a high-context culture, communication is already taking place. Much is said nonverbally, and we need to know that others are already decoding the message inherent in our attitude and facial expressions.

Be self-aware. Knowing your preferred communication style and the manner in which you are likely to enter into communication is an important first step in achieving intercultural communication competence. Your preferred communication style comes not only from your personality but also from your family background and culture. Are you normally aware of the context and usually think before you speak? Do you focus on getting the words right in the message you are trying to share and do not pay attention to your body language? Self-awareness extends to an understanding of how much your feeling of self-worth and your identity is involved in your preferred communication style.

Be observant. One good learning activity is to ask two native speakers to act out giving a gift to each other in various situations. You may ask them to pretend one is a daughter and giving a gift to her mother or one is giving a gift to a sick neighbor. Listen not only for what is said but also observe their body language and other nonverbal behavior. In our culture, we often diminish the gift. We might say, "Here is a little something…it is not much…if you don't like it I can take it back…" People in other cultures may do the opposite. They may go on and on about how expensive the gift was or how much trouble they went to in order to find the right thing. Observing what native speakers say and do in various situations and appropriating their words and behavior will help us communicate effectively.

Be willing to adapt your communication style. Jesus knew what communication style to use with whom. Sometimes He was direct or even confrontational. Often He was indirect, telling stories or using object lessons. He was a master at using the transactional model of communication because His communication was as much about the person He was speaking to as the words He said. He only had to look at Peter after the rooster crowed for the third time, and the message was clear. Some of Jesus's most effective communication occurred when He was silent and refused to answer. With Jesus as our role model, we too should be willing to adapt our communication style to the occasion.

Stacey picked her way along the path, baby Bryan squirming on her back. She tried to arrange a cloth to protect his head from the burning sun, but she still wasn't very skilled at taking care of his needs while he was on her back. She was glad that Muhammad's wife Marie had taught her how to tie the cloth correctly so that Bryan was secure. His chubby legs bounced against her back. Marie and Muhammad's baby girl Anna was now four-months-old. Muhammad had suggested that Stacey take Bryan and sit with his wife in the afternoons while he and Mark went walking in the village. It took so much time cooking and washing clothes, that Stacey could only visit Marie a few times a week. Marie would point to things and say their names which Stacey would repeat. They had even progressed to full sentences. After a few moments, however, Stacey often found herself sitting quietly in the courtyard, playing with Bryan, while Marie went about her tasks. Marie, unlike Muhammad, was one of the few believers in the village. Their marriage had been arranged between their families since they were infants. In spite of Marie's faith, Muhammad had agreed to marry her. Even though Stacey and Marie could barely communicate, Stacey knew that Marie was her friend. It was humbling to realize that even though she had traveled thousands of miles, confident in her abilities, that she was actually the learner and Marie was the teacher. Stacey shook her head. She had so much to learn, so much more than simply learning the language.

Resources:

Gudykunst, W. B. (Ed.). (2005). *Theorizing about intercultural communication.* Thousand Oaks, CA: Sage.

Jandt, F. E. (2004). *An introduction to intercultural communication: Identities in a global community* (4th ed.). Thousand Oaks, CA: Sage.

Tian, J. (2010). A comparative study of Chinese and American cultural context and the influence on communication. *Journal of Language Teaching and Research, 1*, 524-526. doi:10.4304/jltr.1.4.524-526

CHAPTER 4

Learning

Mark shut his computer. Midnight. Where did the time go? Not for the first time, he tried to imagine what life would be like without access to the Internet. Though it had taken several months to have it installed, unless the electricity were off, he had 24-hour access. Of course, that also meant that when he booted up his computer in the morning his parents saw he was online and would pop in on Skype to chat for a while. It wasn't easy to be absorbed into their world and be told about his siblings and nieces and nephews only to realize that a great distance still separated them. On Bryan's birthday, they had let him open his presents where his grandparents could see him on screen. Video chats with his parents were usually followed by the nagging realization that their lives were growing more and more different. His parents were already worried about Bryan's schooling. Stacey was an accomplished accountant, but she had never been trained as a teacher. Thank goodness Bryan could always take online classes. Mark turned out the light to the tiny office, determined not to think about the unknown. Bryan was only one, after all. He was just glad they had already started saving for Bryan's college.

~

The Stories We Heard in School

Remember when you were in third grade and your social studies homework consisted of copying the definitions of vocabulary words from the glossary in the back of your textbook? If only defining everything were as easy as turning to a glossary. Unfortunately, "experts" disagree on how to measure or define many concepts. Those studying topics in areas such as math, chemistry, physics, and biology have an easier time. In those subjects, there is a certain amount of uniformity. People can agree that four plus four equals eight. A tomato plant can be diagrammed. Though there are still many questions as to how our bodies work, enough is known that surgeons can operate on people without having to know their stories. If surgeons need to remove a gall bladder, they do not have to ask where the patient grew up. They just start cutting because they know where to look.

For topics in the social sciences where people's behavior or their interactions in society are studied, defining concepts can be difficult. History, psychology, sociology, education, criminology, anthropology, and communication are just some examples of the social sciences. Whenever we start studying people, things can get fuzzy because people's behavior is based on their background. Since the "experts" who study behavior also come from particular backgrounds, experts in the social sciences often disagree on how to define or describe concepts.

The history recorded in textbooks is written from a particular point of view. If, for example, our U.S. American history books had been written by American Indians, would the text have been different? Though most can agree that certain historical events occurred, such as the Revolutionary War, people in one culture may view the event differently than another. A U. S. American's view of the Revolutionary War is perhaps different from a Briton's view. When we study people, it helps to understand their worldview assumptions and their stories.

The concept of learning has been discussed for centuries. While the results of learning may be obvious, understanding what happens in the learning process is more difficult. Experts disagree on how to describe that process. Much depends upon one's worldview assumptions about knowledge.

Some believe that we are born with certain innate knowledge and abilities that naturally develop. Some believe that for development, a nurturing environment is more important. This controversy over whether one is born with abilities or abilities are developed in the environment is called the nature versus nurture controversy. Many psychologists today believe that as nature and nurture intertwine in development, it is impossible to single out one or the other to explain one's behavior. However, different learning theories and views of education can generally be traced to one or the other side of the controversy. What one believes can influence how one approaches childrearing or learning. Do children's' thoughts naturally become more complex as they age? Do children automatically pick up the language they hear around them because of some innate ability to comprehend language? Or, is it the parent's responsibility to introduce more complex topics and teach language to their children? Does the place and manner in which we learn language impact our results? Nature enthusiasts tend to group people by abilities and ascribe hierarchies. Nurture enthusiasts emphasize experiences, often tracing adult behavior to childhood experiences.

Though we all passed our childhood attending school in some form or the other, it is possible that we have not thought a lot about the schooling process itself. How our schools are organized, how a classroom is arranged, and how teaching in a classroom is conducted often depends upon nature or nurture assumptions. Throughout the world, schools pass along culture as much as they teach special knowledge. Many learning theories have to do with the creation, accommodation, adjustment, or transformation of our cognitive schemata through education.

In the field of education, tension exists between two educational philosophies. One is a linear learning philosophy often called "traditional" and the other is a meaning-based philosophy called "constructivist" in which emphasis is placed on the student understanding process. In our discussion of oral cultures, we noted that knowledge is broken into categories and shared in the community by specialists. Apprentices learn this knowledge or skill and pass it along. Learning becomes teacher-centered as knowledge is transmitted from one "expert" to another. In many collectivistic cultures, the teacher's responsibility is to teach, and the student's responsibility is to learn.

In traditional classrooms in individualistic literate cultures, students focus on basic skills as they master parts that will eventually become elements of more complex wholes. Textbooks are written by "experts," and curriculums determine what each grade will learn. Teachers are often required to stick to the curriculum. Teachers are the authorities who share information, and students are graded on whether they know the "right" answer.

In constructivist classrooms, the emphasis is on big concepts as the curriculum is usually taught beginning with a complex whole that is broken into smaller parts. For example, a "big idea" may be patterns. As students go about their school day, they are encouraged to see patterns in sentences as they study literature, patterns in math, and patterns in biology. In this model, teachers facilitate learning, and students are encouraged to rely on their experience and question what they are learning. Creativity and understanding concepts are prized over repeating information. There is an emphasis on research and "learning how to learn." Change can be equated with progress.

Many U.S. American Christians are unaware of the influence of humanism in our public education system. In 1933, a Humanist Manifesto was signed by more than 30 professors and community leaders. The manifesto, which can be found online, details among other things that the universe was not created and that the religious ideals of previous generations do not meet individuals' needs today. The manifesto declared that humanity's purpose is self-fulfillment and the quest for a good life. One of the signers of this manifesto was John Dewey. Dewey was influential in American education. He emphasized the need for students to interact with their environments in order to learn and meet their potential. He was one of the first constructivist theorists and encouraged teachers to balance their time between sharing information and giving their students opportunities to discover things on their own. As mentioned earlier, in the U.S. communication model, we tend to separate the message from the messenger. For many, Dewey's beliefs about God are separate from his beliefs about education. His beliefs have influenced our education system, however, as fulfilling self is triumphed over pleasing God.

Critics of constructivism note that it is linked with the U.S. American value of individualism, a concept that is often equated with development and modernization (Bowers, 2005). They note that U.S. American culture is tied to consumerism where people are encouraged to buy the next new thing, and products are not expected to endure. Nations that have been deemed "undeveloped" may look for help from the United States in "modernizing" their schools. The resulting "help" may actually lead to an emphasis on individualism and U. S. American cultural values such as personal fulfillment and freedom of choice as well as consumerism. As we have seen previously, individualistic values and collectivistic values often oppose each other. In the push for modernization, schools in countries with a strong oral or collectivistic tradition may take on a constructivist flair. Children who attend those schools may receive individualist messages that conflict with their upbringing.

In the United States today, a mixture of traditional and constructivist ideologies operate in our schools, and teachers are often caught in the middle. With the rise of technology, proponents of constructivism argue that it is more important that students learn how to gather knowledge themselves rather than spend time learning facts. Teachers are encouraged to differentiate their teaching by meeting each student's learning needs. Teaching children to fish takes more time than giving them fish, however. With only so many hours in a school day, it is difficult for many teachers to know how best to balance the time. Often teachers are held accountable for covering the established curriculum. Children are tested on whether they know the "right" answers, and teachers are judged based on their students' testing results.

As cross-cultural workers, we do not arrive at our places of service as blank slates (Lingenfelter & Lingenfelter, 2003). From pre-school, we have been socialized by our culture. When I was learning to read, I was given worksheets in kindergarten with three or four objects arranged in a row. I was told to circle the one that was different. A kindergarten child in China, given the same worksheet, may have been told to circle the objects that were the same. If two children in my preschool class started fighting, the teacher would intervene and probably isolate one or both of them. In Japanese preschools, children who disagree are usually left to work it out for themselves and are not made examples before the group. There, teachers often model conversations that children might have, acceptable ways to respond, if conflict arises (Tobin, Wu, & Davidson, 1989).

In individualistic cultures such as in the United States, sometimes there is the assumption that knowledge shared through schools has been through the rigors of scientific testing and is "neutral." This knowledge, published in textbooks or academic journals, is shared with students who must show that they have mastered it in order to "pass." The most valid knowledge is often seen as that which is shared in such formal settings. As the federal government gains more and more influence in local education, schools are taking over responsibilities that previously only parents had. With the humanistic emphasis in our culture and in our schools, parents need to be as wise as serpents.

In many other cultures, valid knowledge is knowledge that has been tested through time and has been passed from generation to generation. Whereas there is little place for the spiritual in U. S. American public education, many other cultures recognize a spiritual element to knowledge and learning.

As Christian workers, understanding the influence that our schooling has had on our beliefs about learning and education should have us running for our Bibles. Though it is impossible to interpret Scripture except through our own worldview, once we are aware of the powerful cultural stories that have influenced us, we are in a better position to question our actions. Otherwise, we may unwittingly believe that all our behavior is biblical rather than influenced by our cultural heritage.

Adult Learners

Adults are always learning, though when asked, many may have difficulty describing a learning experience. Because we spent our formative years in school, many of us confuse schooling with learning. However, as adults, most of our learning does not take place in the confines of a formal program but informally as a part of daily life. Whether it is a new route to work or a new recipe, we are constantly interacting with the world around us. When problems arise, we seek a solution. We can enroll in workshops offered by local home improvement stores to learn how to tile a bathroom. We can take a night course at the local community college and learn how to do our taxes. We can read a magazine article on how to understand our grandchildren. Unless our job requires continuing education, we can schedule our own learning as it fits our needs. If we need to know something now, we do not like to wait.

As adults, we are conscious that the world is getting smaller. Globalization affects adult learning. Globalization is the movement of goods, people, and culture across national boundaries. Communication technology and the Internet have encouraged globalization. Some believe that we have passed from an industrial society to a knowledge society (Merriam & Bierema, 2014). Though machines are still important, the knowledge that allows one to produce more efficient machines is of more value than the machine itself. People often seek knowledge and education in order to fulfill personal goals.

Malcolm Knowles (2012), an educational theorist, proposed a theory of adult learning in the late 1960s called andragogy. Frustrated by his efforts to understand more about adult learning, Knowles realized that adults were being taught in the same way as children. He began to study ways in which teaching adults, andragogy, is different from teaching children, pedagogy.

Knowles theorized that adults view themselves as self-directed learners. Adults are ready to learn when they need to know something and often engage in learning when they need to solve a problem. Their experience, among other things, sets them apart from children and provides a learning resource.

Critics have said that andragogy describes adult learning in individualistic cultures and does not necessarily apply to adult learning in all cultures (Merriam & Bierema, 2014). However, it has been found that many adults in oral cultures also engage in self-directed learning. When a problem arises, rather than looking for answers in books or on the Internet, they seek out other people who can help or teach them (Field, 1977).

We tend to teach in the same manner that we were taught. If we grew up as a student in traditional classrooms, we may believe that the correct way to teach is to be an authoritarian teacher. Unless we are teaching children, however, we will probably experience difficulty. Even in individualistic cultures, interaction is an important element when working with adults. Interaction is also important in oral, collectivistic cultures. In higher education in collectivistic cultures, teachers may have a traditional role in the classroom. Students may be taught that to question the teacher or to offer their own ideas is rude because it wastes other students' time, time they could be learning from the teacher. Outside the classroom, however, teachers often take on a parental role with a more relaxed relationship with their students.

Jesus taught in an oral, collectivistic culture yet his message was not only to groups but to individuals. Those of us from an individualistic culture can learn a lot by looking at Jesus' teaching style.

Jesus' Teaching Style

We know that Jesus was literate because he read from the scrolls in the synagogue. However, he did not leave a book behind to explain his message or ministry. Jesus taught using oral instructional methods, especially modeling. Jesus was well-versed in both direct and indirect communication. He was a master in using stories, pithy statements, proverbs, and object lessons. Sometimes he spoke so indirectly that his disciples had difficulty understanding him. Jesus often spoke directly to his disciples, however, explaining parables or the purpose behind his actions.

Perhaps Jesus' greatest teaching method was modeling. Though he was familiar with the synagogue schools of that day, he did not choose that method to teach his disciples, for Jesus' teaching was not confined to a place. He taught in the synagogues, on hillsides, in courtyards, and in homes. Jesus had a strong relationship with his disciples. He did not set appointments to meet with them to discuss a lesson for an hour or two. Instead, they lived together. His disciples saw him draw apart to pray. They saw him heal. They saw him teach the crowds and yet saw him also deal individually with the disciples themselves. Jesus knew his disciples and adjusted his teaching according to their needs.

Jesus used silence as a communication tool. Once, he busied himself writing in the sand while accusers waited for an answer. He only had to look at Peter after the rooster had crowed for a third time, and Peter got the message. He refused to answer his accusers during his trial.

Jesus held his followers accountable for teaching others what they had learned. Jesus sent his disciples out into the world to practice what he had taught them. Upon their return they reported to him for his comments. He told his disciples that they were to entrust to faithful men the responsibility of passing along what they had seen and heard. According to the Bible, Jesus frequently gave oral exams, questioning his disciples as to their understanding, watching their behavior, correcting them when needed.

Once, in a discussion of the importance of local Bible schools, my husband asked our African pastor why he felt strongly that pastors needed to spend time at a Bible school with their families before taking responsibility for a church. Our pastor replied that as outsiders, when we have training meetings with local pastors, we can be easily fooled as to the men's character as they might tell us the answers we want to hear. We do not see how they interact with their families or their neighbors. "Put these men in close quarters for a while with their wives and children, and it won't be long before you know who has regular devotions, who mistreats his wife, who can't get along with his neighbor, or who doesn't discipline his children. In that situation, more mature believers can come alongside and model biblical behavior. The wives, also, have a chance to be discipled by older women at the moment an issue arises. This older pastor often had one or two young pastors living with him in his courtyard as he modeled Christian living.

For those of us in individualistic cultures, modeling can be difficult. Modeling involves sacrificing personal freedom and being available when we are needed. Often, we prefer the transmission communication model. Too often, our idea of discipleship is giving someone a book. We hesitate to ask too many questions. It is possible that we fear that if we hold others accountable for their actions, then they will also hold us accountable. What will happen to our personal freedom, then?

It is difficult, but not impossible, to teach and to model cross-culturally. In order to be successful, at least three things must happen. First, we must know ourselves. We must examine our beliefs and actions in light of Scripture. We must look into our pasts, the stories we were told, and consciously identify areas in which our cognitive schemata need to be adjusted or transformed. We must also realize that God did not make a mistake when he created us. Though we may pick up some collectivistic understandings, many of us will always be an individualist at heart. God knows when our skin crawls because the person who came to see us will not get to the point and the million things we had planned to accomplish that day are tugging at our mind. As Americans, we tend to draw an imaginary line at our neck when we say we are "fed up." I like where the French draw their imaginary line. It is over their head. Many times, I have felt that the imaginary line that divides where I can or cannot "take any more" has reached to the top of my head. It is okay. God knows.

Second, we must help those we are trying to teach to examine their beliefs and actions in light of Scripture. What are they currently doing that even though strange to us, does not violate Scripture? If it does not violate Scripture but violates our individualistic cultural beliefs, how are we going to respond? If their cultural practices do violate Scripture, how do we lead them to replace those practices with other behaviors that are Scriptural and will help meet their needs?

Third, we must be willing to be transparent. We cannot ask them to change if we are not willing to change ourselves. We must give them the privilege of holding us accountable just as we are holding them accountable. It is not easy to look at our own actions through their eyes. Once, I was asked to sing a solo before our African congregation. Just as I got to the chorus, the African preacher's wife got up from her seat and came up to the podium next to me. She held a small toy camera. As I was trying to sing, she leaned in close, pretending to take a picture. She walked all around me, holding the camera at various angles. It was difficult to concentrate on my song. Eventually, I got through it. However, at the end of the song, everyone in the congregation, including myself, were laughing at her antics. She was mimicking the behavior that she had seen from us as well as from volunteers. Though she was exaggerating what she had seen, she made her point. That is the beauty of oral teaching methods. She did not have to say anything. After that, I reminded our volunteers that even though the African worship service was different from the one they experienced in the States, it was still a worship service. If they did not want someone walking up and down the aisle in their home church to get a good picture angle, they should not do that in an African service, either. I have to admit, I was much more respectful as well.

In the next part, you will have an opportunity to do the hard work of examining the stories that define you. Now that you are aware of the awesome power of stories in how we think, communicate, and learn, you can use that knowledge to investigate the influence stories have had on you personally.

~

The creaking of the front gate brought Mark from his reverie. Muhammad ambled up the path as Mark got up from the couch. Calling to Stacey, he opened the screen door. He didn't even look at his watch. He wouldn't have been able to look at it if he had wanted to, for his watch was safely stored in a box in the dresser. He had learned that it were better for his blood pressure if he did not wear a watch while they were in the village. Mark had to admit, the days took on a certain tranquility, a certain rhythm. He exchanged greetings with Muhammad as Stacey entered the room. She led Bryan, walking hesitantly behind her. She reached for the box of building blocks she kept in the corner and sat Bryan beside them. "How is Marie?" she asked, "and Anna?"

"They are well. She is always happy when you go to visit her. She said to tell you that she is visiting her aunt this afternoon, the one who just got back from the hospital. If you want to go with her, you are welcome. I think it would be a good opportunity for you to practice your language."

"That would be great. Tell her I will be by after Bryan wakes up from his nap," Stacey replied. Mark picked up the notebook stuffed with language notes from the couch.

"Where do you think we should begin?" he asked Muhammad.

"We were talking yesterday about the fact that we need more government jobs. Only a few of us were able to go to university. I am lucky that I found work with the government radio station, but others are not so lucky. Unemployment is a big problem."

"I have noticed a lot of young men hanging around downtown," Mark replied. "Is there nothing for them to do?"

"No," Muhammad shook his head sadly. "The government pushes education but since there is no high school in our village, the students who wish to go to high school have to go somewhere else. Then, after all that work, they return home, and there are no jobs."

"I suppose they could work in the fields with their parents..." Stacey began.

"No way," Muhammad interrupted her. "After all that education, they deserve better. They are not interested in working in the fields, and I don't blame them. Like I said, we need more government jobs."

Resources:

Bowers, C. A. (2005). The false promises of constructivist theories of learning: A global and ecological critique. New York, NY: Peter Lang Academic.

Field, J. L. (1977). The learning efforts of Jamaican adults of low literacy attainment (Doctoral dissertation). Retrieved from ProQuest UMI dissertations publishing. (NK36646)

Knowles, M. S., Holton, E. F., & Swanson, R. A. (2012). The adult learner: The definitive classic in adult education and human resource development (7th ed.). New York, NY: Routledge.

Lingenfelter, J. E., & Lingenfelter, S. G. (2003). Teaching cross-culturally: An incarnational model for learning and teaching. Grand Rapids, MI: Baker Academic.

Merriam, S. B., & Bierema, L. L. (2014). Adult learning: Linking theory and practice. San Francisco, CA: Jossey-Bass.

Tobin, J. J., Wu, D. Y. H., & Davidson, D. H. (1989). Preschool in three cultures: Japan, China, and the United States. New Haven, CT: Yale University Press.

Part II

Understanding the Stories that Define Us

CHAPTER 5

Personal Stories

Stacey took one last look at the table, trying to ignore Bryan's cries from the other room. "Mark, she called, "Will you please get him. I do not have much time, and I'm really busy here." Mark appeared in the doorway, a sullen Bryan in his arms.

"What are you so worried about?" he asked as he nodded his head toward the table laden with food. "You've been in the kitchen all morning. I doubt if they're expecting all this."

"That is not the point," Stacey said sharply. "These are the first guests we've had for a meal. Even if they won't be here very long, I want everything to be just right."

"But it's only John and Joyce. John said on the phone they just want to stop in to see how we're doing." Stacey straightened the edge of the satin tablecloth and grimaced at the wilting flowers.

"I don't care. If something needs doing, it is worth doing right." Mark shook his head, then turned toward the front door as he heard a car drive up.

"Whatever," he said, and headed toward the front door with a fussing Bryan in tow. Stacey did not want to get in an argument when they were about to have guests. She waved a fly away from the mashed potatoes. Perhaps it was not exactly like her mother would have done it, but Stacey was satisfied. Exhausted, but satisfied.

In Part I, we discussed cognitive schemata, culture schema theory, collectivistic and individualistic cultures, communication theories, adult learning, and other topics that help us understand ourselves and our world. In Part II, we want to better understand the stories that define us. As we have learned, each of us is unique with a unique background. We all have different stories. Because our backgrounds are different, comparing our story to someone else's is not always beneficial. We can better understand our actions and beliefs, however, by examining what we were told as a child, the stories we heard at home as well as the stories we heard at school. I do not mean the fairy tales or children's books that were read to us. I am referring to those stories that we either overheard adults tell each other or the stories we saw lived out by the adults around us. Each of us is the main character in our story. In all good stories, there must be conflict. What are the conflicts in your story? What were the inadvertent lessons you learned about yourself or others?

Just thinking about our personal stories is not enough. We need a framework which will help us understand and possibly alter the stories that define us and others. In this first section, I review a skill called "critical thinking." This skill is not only helpful in reviewing past experiences, it is a necessary skill for dealing with the issues we all face daily. After reviewing critical thinking, I discuss ways in which critical thinking can aid us in problem solving, especially in solving relationship issues when unique personal stories cause conflicting behaviors.

Critical Thinking

Critical thinking can be defined in various ways. The best definition is in the term itself, for critical thinking basically means purposely thinking critically. Critical thinking is linked to purposeful thinking, problem solving, and creativity.

We need to think critically about our speech, actions, beliefs, relationships, problems, decisions – basically, everything that happens in our lives. We learned about the purpose of schemata in Part I. Schemata provide us with "stories" or "scripts" that once established, allow us to go through life seemingly without thinking. On the one hand, we need schemata so that we do not have to stop and think about everything.

If you had to purposely think about every step involved in driving whenever you need to go somewhere, driving would become a slow and laborious process. My husband taught our children to drive because he has more patience than I. He sat calmly beside them as they thought about the steps involved in putting the car in motion. I would have said, "Just turn the key already!" Years later, the act of driving is automatic for our children, but they had to develop a driving schema. Critical thinking involves stopping and examining a schema instead of acting automatically. We ask ourselves why we are saying, deciding, behaving, or believing such a thing.

Examining a schema is hard work. Sometimes it is easier to "go with the flow." Have you ever heard someone say, "Don't think so much?" Sometimes, when we are building a schema, for example, too much thinking can get in the way. If someone is in that space between learning a new skill and practicing the skill, yet cannot quite leave the learning stage, they may be advised, "don't think so much." That advice can often be heard in sports where instead of trusting one's training and just swinging the golf club or shooting the basketball, one begins to "think too much" with disastrous consequences. Too much thinking is sometimes a detriment when learning a new language. If we are always thinking about what we are going to say, it may mean that we are still speaking our first language in our heads.

Sometimes, you may hear, "I just don't want to think about it too much." In this situation, there may be an unwillingness to face the facts of a situation or consider the consequences of our actions. For a Christian, not "thinking about it too much" may mean knowing God wants us to change something about ourselves and being unwilling to do so. Though we need to develop schemata that allow us to move easily through life, sometimes stopping and thinking before we do something is necessary. Often, our automatic reaction to a situation is not always the best reaction.

Some of the best childrearing advice I received was not to say "no" automatically when I was busy and my children interrupted me, asking to do something. This advice, from a magazine article I read years ago, was in the form of a story. A young mother explained that one day she was cleaning house for a party that evening when her young sons asked if they could put water in the bathtub and play with their boats. The mother's automatic reaction to this request was to say "no" because she wanted a clean house and her sons' request would surely mean water on the bathroom floor. She said, however, she stopped rushing around and seriously thought about their request. She realized that agreeing to let them play with their boats meant her sons would be happily occupied for a long time. She would be free to continue her house cleaning in peace. Also, she would have to mop the bathroom eventually. Some water on the floor would actually help her. After thinking, she let them play with their boats in the bathtub. Her story stuck with me, as stories tend to do.

Critical thinking means stopping, purposely thinking, and critically examining ourselves or a situation. Critical thinking has also been linked to reasoning, thinking logically, or problem solving. Children in Western schools are taught to think critically, though they may not realize that is what they are learning. School children are taught to look at a problem as a whole then break a big problem into smaller, solvable, steps. In language arts, for example, they are taught to consider the meaning or the theme of the whole text. They then discuss the text by paragraphs, looking for the theme of each paragraph. In understanding how to do word problems in math, they are taught to look at the whole problem first. Then, they are taught to look for signal phrases such as "how many are left" that serve as markers and will tell them whether they need to add, subtract, multiply, or divide.

This skill of breaking a larger problem into smaller pieces is useful throughout life. It is especially helpful when a problem or situation seems "too big" and threatens to be overwhelming. By breaking the problem into steps and beginning on the steps that are within our capabilities, the problem may not seem so large.

Another part of critical thinking that is taught to children is learning how to look at a problem from different angles. Children are often given mazes on paper and asked to draw their way through the maze without becoming blocked. They soon learn to work backwards or look at the maze from different sides instead of beginning to work the maze and find their way through trial and error. This type of critical thinking is often linked to creativity. One needs to be creative to see a problem in a new light. A popular creativity test is to ask someone how many ways a brick can be used. The more "out of the box" responses, the more creative the person is deemed to be.

Often, when we are overwhelmed by situations or are advising someone else who is overwhelmed, we need to remember the problem solving skills we learned in school. We need to look at the problem as a whole, then break it into solvable parts. We may need to look at it from a different direction and be creative. We may need to look at "signal phrases" that can help us determine what to do. Proverbs 14:15 says, "A simple man believes anything, but a prudent man gives thought to his steps." As Christians, we are told to be prudent and to think.

Critical thinking for adults goes beyond critical thinking as it is taught to children. Though for adults, critical thinking also includes thinking purposefully, problem solving, and being creative, critical thinking for adults includes questioning our assumptions.

Trust the Story

As mentioned in Part I, one way in which adults differ from children is that adults have much more life experience and bring their experience to each learning situation. With that experience comes certain assumptions, conclusions that we have drawn about ourselves or others. We may not know where those assumptions came from or even that they exist. Just like schemata, our assumptions usually remain unquestioned. These assumptions are a part of our worldview.

According to one writer (Brookfield, 2012), critical thinking for adults consists of four easy steps. In any situation in which we need to think critically, we need to first hunt the assumptions in that situation. Hunting the assumptions means not only hunting our assumptions but others' assumptions as well. The second step is to check the assumption. Is our assumption true? Is theirs? The third step is to look at the assumption from others' points of view, and the fourth step is to decide on a course of action.

Going through these steps is especially helpful when we are faced with messages from the media. In one television commercial, a popular male star entices the audience to switch from cable to his preferred television provider. In the commercial, this star also plays a person who has cable, a person who is inept socially with limited finances. The star tells the audience not to be like the one who has cable but to be like him, the star, who has the other television provider. Engaging in critical thinking, it is easy to see the assumptions in this commercial. By linking the star with one television provider and the inept individual with cable, the assumption the commercial is trying to sell is that "if you want to be like a star, choose the television provider he does..." If we check that assumption, we can easily see where it is false. If we look at the assumption from others' points of view, not to mention the people the commercial makes fun of, again we see that the assumption is false, for many people are perfectly happy with cable television. What should be our informed plan of action? My personal plan is to purposely resist the message this commercial, this story, is trying to feed me each time I see it.

These critical thinking steps often need to be adjusted for the Christian. In the second step, a non-Christian's definition of "truth," and the Christian's definition are not necessarily the same. The non-Christian may decide something is true if it "feels right," or if it agrees with "scientific reasoning." For Christians, when we come to the second step of checking the assumptions, we need to ask, "Does this assumption line up with the Word of God and what I know about who God is?"

The third step of looking at our assumptions from others' points of view is critical for the Christian as well. Worldviews vary. Are we assuming that others look at the world in the same way as we? It does not mean that we have to accept others' assumptions if their assumptions differ from ours. However, knowing how others arrived at their assumptions allows us to be more understanding.

The fourth and last step of making an informed plan of action can be as simple as deciding not to act based on our newfound understanding. For Christians, it should also include looking to God for His solution. Does He want us to act? Does He want us to wait? To keep silent? To speak?

Critical thinking is a necessary part of learning to solve problems. For those in collectivistic cultures, especially oral cultures, their problems are often of the human variety. In such a culture, individuals do not normally walk away from the group. They have to learn to get along. They learn to compromise. They learn that they cannot always express their emotions in the way they wish. People in collectivistic cultures do not always live together as one happy family, however. Just as in individualistic cultures, people have family members, work colleagues, or neighbors who have strong personalities or lack social skills. In collectivistic cultures, however, such individuals tend to realize that if they want to be part of the group, they need to change. In individualistic cultures, if there is someone who gets on our nerves, we tend to avoid that person. If we are part of a group and are not satisfied with the way the group is functioning, we often leave the group. Unfortunately, the person or other people in the group may never know the reason why we are pulling away.

In my opinion, in individualistic cultures, we may get very good at solving abstract problems but many times we do not have experience solving relationship problems. If we are used to walking away from relationship problems, difficulties arise when we are in a situation, such as on the mission field, when we cannot easily walk away from others.

To engage in critical thinking when we encounter relationship problems, we follow the first step of hunting assumptions. To hunt assumptions often means to go back to the childhood stories of those involved in the situation. We then need to check these assumptions against the Word of God and try to see the assumption from the other's point of view. Lastly, we need to take informed action – which may mean only nodding our head in increased understanding.

This fictional story is an example of how critical thinking can be applied to a relationship issue on the mission field. A newly-arrived young couple began asking an older couple to babysit their young children. The older couple did not mind babysitting occasionally, but it appeared the younger couple expected them to agree whenever the younger couple wished. Conflict began to grow as the older couple had a difficult time saying, "No," yet complained to others about their frustration as the younger couple asked the older couple to babysit more and more. Before the situation got out of hand, another field representative asked if both couples would sit down for a meeting. The field representative outlined the situation then helped both couples engage in critical thinking by first asking the younger couple to identify their assumptions. The younger couple were used to dropping their children by their grandparent's house in the States whenever they wanted. They assumed the older couple would want to watch their children and were mentally putting the older couple in the role of substitute grandparents. The field representative asked the older couple if they saw themselves in this role. Unused to confronting their issues in this way, the older couple admitted, rather uncomfortably, that they did not see themselves in this role and that several times they had planned to go visiting but stayed at home instead to watch the younger couple's children. When the younger couple's assumptions were checked, they were seen to be false. The younger couple put themselves in the older couple's place and realized that babysitting their children was limiting the older couple's ability to engage in ministry and do as they wished. The older couple put themselves in the younger couple's place and realized the younger couple needed time alone without their children. The field representative asked both couples to develop an informed plan of action. The older couple gave a limited number of babysitting coupons to the younger couple. When the younger couple felt they needed time alone, the younger couple called the older couple and asked if it were convenient to use one of their coupons. By hunting and checking the assumptions, seeing the assumptions from others' points of view, and developing an informed plan of action, conflict was avoided and both couples' needs were met.

Critical thinking is a useful tool for solving problems. We should understand the difference between critical thinking and critical theory, however. Critical theory is a field of study in which many proponents charge, among other things, that people can be kept from realizing their "potential" by their belief systems. While some concepts in critical theory are useful for reflection, such as the way we use language to categorize others, be aware that the assumptions of critical theory and Christian beliefs can differ. Be sure to engage in critical thinking when it comes to critical theory.

Personal stories

Understanding critical thinking gives us a plan of action and a way to approach looking at our personal stories. If only it were as simple as holding personal stories up to the light of critical thinking, however. Stories are so powerful, that sometimes, even when we subject them to critical thinking, their power does not fade. I call these stories, "the voices in our head," because they are often associated with a person in our memory.

Trust the Story

One year, about the middle of August, I flew from Africa to the United States for a conference. I packed lightly. The only shoes I took were a pair of white sandals. Everything was fine, until I had to extend my time in the States. The closer it got to the first Monday in September, the more nervous I became. Though my mother had died many years previously, I still had her voice in my head. As a Southerner, she had taught me that a lady never wears white shoes after Labor Day. I did not want to spend money on another pair of shoes. I had only found one brand that stood up to the rocky rigors of Africa, and they were expensive. The first Monday of September came and went. I told myself that the "story" my mother had told me was old-fashioned, that no one abided by that maxim anymore. I kept repeating how ridiculous it was to buy another pair of shoes right up to the time I walked in the shoe store and bought a pair of black sandals. I told the clerk sheepishly, "I'm only doing this because of my mother's voice in my head." The clerk was too young to have heard of the "no white shoes after Labor Day" prohibition. She was just happy I was spending so much money. I left the store feeling foolish yet satisfied. My mother would have been proud.

What are the stories in your head? What were you told when you were a child that influences your behavior to this day? Perhaps you were told stories about what boys or girls should do when they grow up. White picket fence, married, two children and a dog, anyone? Perhaps you heard many positive stories. I remember as a four-year-old sitting at the feet of my grandmother as she taught the ladies in Women's Missionary Union, listening to her stories of missionaries in Africa. I believe God used that experience to later nudge me toward the calling He had for me. I was blessed to come from a Christian family where our faith was taken seriously. I often heard stories of God's provision and the need to follow His will.

Your experience may have been similar or very different. Take a few moments and consider the stories you were told when you were young. How does your behavior reflect those stories? Who told you those stories? Use critical thinking to examine those stories. What were the assumptions that were illustrated in the stories you were told? Are those assumptions in line with the Word of God? Do you understand where those assumptions came from? Were they assumptions that had been passed down from generation to generation but never held to the light of God's Word? What is your plan of action? As I illustrated in the story of the white shoes, it is not always easy to let go of personal stories. In my example, as silly as it was, the story was not something that adversely affected my life. I knew I would wear the black sandals and eventually get my money's worth. However, there may be stories that you have believed that are negatively impacting you. Perhaps, you are telling others those same negative stories. Hunt your assumptions. Check them in the light of God's Word. Understand how others may have come to their assumptions. Make a plan of how you might need to change.

U.S. American Cultural Stories

In a book aimed at helping international students understand U. S. American culture, Stan Nussbaum (2005) examines popular sayings that demonstrate our cultural beliefs. He identified ten major U.S. American values. This is the way he described them:

1. **Success**. Success is the greatest U. S. American value. People desire the "American dream" which they believe can be obtained through hard work, cleverness, self-confidence, and ambition.

2. **Tolerance, privacy, and freedom**. People want to be left alone to live however they wish and do whatever they want. They believe others should be tolerant of their desires.

3. **Fun**. Children should be allowed to play, and learning should be fun. Adults seek fun jobs, or if that is not possible, have a hobby or participate in a sport in order to have fun. People cannot wait to retire so they can have more fun.

4. **Shopping**. The process of shopping is a form of recreation.

5. **Action**. Rather than getting permission, people prefer to act on their ideas.

6. **Youth**. Youth is to be enjoyed, a time free from adult responsibilities.

7. **Rights**. People have rights and should stand up for themselves. They should not allow others to interfere with their rights.

8. **Autonomy**. People should think for themselves and break the rules if they have to.

9. **Time**. As a value, time is money and can be wasted.

10. **Hard work**. Hard work is believed to be the key to obtaining success.

Whether or not we agree with Nussbaum's conclusions, it is easy to see how each of these values has impacted us. If you were to go down the list, can you think of a "story" that you were told as a child, or are still hearing now, that affirms each of these values? Nussbaum considers the top U.S. American value to be success. How do we gauge success? Possibly, in the secular world, success is measured by the size of one's bank account. Because we value autonomy, we generally believe that one has the right to decide how his or her money will be spent. U.S. Americans are often surprised to learn that in many African cultures, it is often the person with the need who decides whether the person with the money should respond to the need, especially if both individuals are related. In the Christian world, we often gauge success by "numbers," numbers of converts or the size of a church.

After my husband graduated from seminary, we felt God calling us to move from Texas to Wyoming to be church planters. With the help of a church in the Fort Worth area and a loan from my husband Marvin's parents, we moved to a coal-mining town of 350 people to begin a church. A Baptist church in a neighboring city sponsored us. Many of our church members were new converts. It seemed as if we could never grow the church to more than about 35 to 40 people, however. Just as it looked like we would take off, a family in our congregation would move away in search of work. My husband became discouraged. After several years, we sat down one day and began to count all of the people who had been touched by our ministry, even if they no longer lived in our town. The total came to many more than 35. We realized that we might never reach "success" in church planting as many gauged success. Our church would probably always remain small. Our success was in the number of lives we had touched. It was difficult to adjust our concept of success, however. Perhaps it was because we knew others judged us by the standard view. We were afraid that because of the belief that hard work is rewarded with success, the fact that we did not have a large church made it look as if we were not working.

A beneficial exercise is to look at each of the ten values, then engage in critical thinking. What assumptions go with each value? I mentioned the assumption that goes with the "success" value, that of a large bank account or big numbers – a lot of converts or church members. Because we value cleverness and see that as a component of success, it may be that we also assume that "success" requires sacrifice, either relationships or ethics. Now, we need to check our assumptions. Does success equate a large bank account or a lot of converts? Sometimes, but not always. Now we look at the assumptions through other's viewpoints. In this instance, we need to ask: How does God gauge success? I believe the answer is "obedience." What is our informed plan of action? We must seek to be obedient, not only be obedient to God and what we believe He is asking of us but also to those in authority over us.

Engage in critical thinking for each of the remaining values. Hunt and check the assumptions. Explore God's Word asking what Scripture says about each value and its corresponding assumptions. What is your plan of action?

Personality Development

We have discussed the powerful way in which our larger cultural stories influence us. One development theory, ecological systems theory which was proposed by Urie Bronfenbrenner (1981), emphasizes how an individual, nestled at the center of layer upon layer of relationship systems, is influenced by decisions that others make in those outer layers. We may not be personally involved in those systems but their indirect influence still impacts our lives.

The outer relationship layer which impacts us is not only our larger culture but also any group of which we are a part that has its own culture. Every organization that has been in existence very long develops its own culture, its unwritten procedures and unstated beliefs. Decisions made in those relationship layers, even though we may never be personally involved in that layer, necessarily impacts us as individuals.

My father was a sergeant in the Air Force. My mother loved the military culture and enjoyed the security that being in the Air Force can bring. It was a new experience when my father was transferred to Germany, and my whole family pulled up our Texas roots and traveled to Europe. I believe God used that first cross-cultural experience to prepare me for the life He had for me. Decisions made in a military office to move my father to Germany impacted me.

I do not believe that the decisions made in the outer relationship layers that surround us are random, however, but orchestrated by God. It is overwhelming to realize all that God does to put us in the "right" place at the "right" time. It is not always about us, however. A colleague once told me that she did not know how effective she was on the mission field (she was very effective) but as her children grew, she realized that God called her and her husband because He wanted their children to grow up on the mission field.

Have you ever traced the seemingly "random" acts that led you to where you are today? There are many examples in my own life where God intervened miraculously to change my circumstances or put me in the place I needed to be for His next step. I believe that one aspect of faith is not fighting those outer layers but resting securely, nestled at the center of His will as He works out His purposes.

I am conscious that as God works and I am faced with a decision, I always have a choice, to be obedient or disobedient. Others have the same choice. A stranger's choice to rebel against God may have disastrous consequences. A drunk driver takes the life of a young mother. A new Christian is murdered by terrorists. Churches are burned. Though it is difficult to understand why God allows these tragic acts, we can be secure in knowing that nothing is a surprise to Him. We are never outside His control.

Often when we make decisions, we consider the impact the decision will have on us or our family. Like pebbles in a pool of water, however, a decision's impact can ripple out to affect people we have never met. Each decision we make, especially those decisions that impact where we live or what we do, must be made in accordance with God's will. Though it can be easy to see how others' decisions to be disobedient can negatively impact those around them, sometimes we are blind to how our decisions impact others. Not going through the chore of language learning impacts whether or not I can share the gospel. Consistently neglecting our own children's needs to meet the needs of others may influence our children's understanding of God. Not taking care of my emotional needs may mean I am not as effective in relating to others as I should be.

Understanding the personal stories from your culture and your childhood that have impacted you is critical as you consider the Bible stories you will tell in your ministry. It is possible that the stories we choose and the parts of the story we emphasize are influenced by our cultural values. Only recently, in thinking about the Joseph story, have I pondered the many years that Joseph spent in prison. In retrospect, I know I mentioned those years when I told the story on the mission field. However, I usually moved quickly to the end of the story and the success that Joseph achieved. Why did I fail to emphasize the day after day after day of Joseph's prison existence? How often do we think about the times Joseph's hopes must have been raised, the times he thought he was going to be rescued, only to be seemingly forgotten again? In my own life, I want to see God act quickly. I want an immediate answer to my prayers. Would I have been as faithful as Joseph, suffering for years? I have to ask myself, in telling that story in the past, why did I gloss over the many years that Joseph waited for God to come to his rescue? Did I make it sound as if God always responds to our needs quickly? Was I so anxious for a convert (success) that I put less emphasis on the parts of the story that I felt might "discourage" my hearers?

How has your personality been influenced by the layers of relationships surrounding you? How have others' stories intersected with yours to help mold you into who you are today? Are you nestled securely in the center of God's will as He works to fulfill His purposes? Are you aware of God working miraculously around you? These stories of seeing God at work in the layers of your life are your faith stories. In the next chapter, we will discuss the importance of sharing faith stories in your ministry.

"What happened when you went to visit Marie's aunt" asked Mark. "Did you pray for her?" "Yes," said Stacey.

"Great, we can count that." Stacey peered over her husband's shoulder at the computer screen where he was filling out their monthly report.

"Are you sure? It was Marie's idea for me to get more practice in praying in the local language."

"That doesn't matter. You did it. Now, what else? Any other spiritual conversations?"

"I honestly don't remember. I know I should keep track every day, but I forget. I don't know if you can describe what I do as 'conversations' anyway. I know enough of the language to talk but I still have difficulty understanding when people speak to me." Stacey eyed her husband. "You don't need to get so upset about it. These reports are meant to encourage us, or at least they are supposed to."

"I'm just tired of putting zeros by everything." Mark shut the lid of the computer and rubbed his eyes. "I'll finish it tomorrow." He stood up and hugged Stacey close to him. "I understand why we need to learn the language and fill out these reports, but when I do, I'm reminded of what a failure I am. Muhammad is the only one I know who speaks English, and every time I start talking to him about my faith he gets this faraway look in his eyes, and I know he's only listening because I'm paying him. I will be so glad when we pass our language test and can finally get down to work. Remember the success we had in North Carolina?" Mark's voice was wistful. "That was so much fun. It may be a little harder, but I'm ready for that kind of success here. I can't wait to fill in that form with some big numbers! All of this doing nothing is driving me crazy."

Resources:

Bronfenbrenner, U. (1981). *The ecology of human development: Experiments by nature and design.* Cambridge, MA: Harvard University Press.

Brookfield, S. D. (2012). *Teaching for critical thinking: Tools and techniques to help students question their assumptions.* San Francisco, CA: Jossey-Bass.

Nussbaum, S. (2005). *American cultural baggage: How to recognize and deal with it.* Maryknoll, NY: Orbis.

CHAPTER 6

Faith Stories

Mark glanced quickly at the paper in his lap before covering it with his hand, squinting in concentration as he tried to remember what he had written. He grinned. Muhammad did not know it yet, but in his language session this morning, Mark planned to ask Muhammad to listen to his testimony. Muhammad would listen because it was his job to listen, but Mark and Stacey had prayed together that today Muhammad would listen with his heart as well as his head. For several weeks, Mark had been thinking about what he could say, asking Muhammad for vocabulary. If Muhammad understood him, then Mark was planning to repeat his testimony to as many men as would listen as he and Muhammad visited downtown this afternoon. Mark closed his eyes and repeated the words to himself silently. If only he could share in English... As he heard the front gate open, he opened one eye and peeked at the page. He had remembered it correctly. It was going to be a good day.

In this chapter, we will look at our personal faith stories on two levels. The first level is understanding how to use our salvation testimony to impact others and how our choice of words when we share our salvation testimony may actually inhibit others from hearing our message. The second level is becoming conscious of God's daily working in our life and learning how to share that story with others. When we see God's hand, are we reminded of how He worked similarly with someone in the Bible? Is there a particular biblical character with whom you identify? Knowing how to insert stories from God's Word into conversation when we share our personal faith stories is a learned skill. As mentioned previously, all good stories include conflict. Some of the best personal faith stories come from when we struggled with God and limped away from the encounter with renewed faith.

Salvation Testimony

Our salvation testimony is just that – ours. It is a unique story of God's calling us to salvation and our acceptance. Because it is our story, we can choose how to tell it. There is no "right" way. More importantly, we must consider our audience when we tell it. For example, we each have a story of our first job. How we tell that story to a prospective employer and how we tell that story to a good friend will differ. We pick and choose which details to emphasize and which details to leave out. If we do not add details that are not there, whether we tell the story in five minutes with a lot of interesting details or we streamline the story to a minute rendition of the skills we learned, the story is still true. As Christians, we need to become adept at knowing how to adapt our salvation story depending upon our audience.

Our salvation story begins before our testimony of when we actually accepted Christ. It includes how, in retrospect, we can see God's hand moving to put us in the exact spot where we needed to be in order to hear and respond to Him. Too often a Christian's testimony only includes a summary of the gospel. Though the gospel is a beautiful story of God's love and redemption and sharing the gospel is necessary, our salvation story is unique. The gospel is an integral part of our salvation story, but our story extends to more than the gospel. It also includes the working of God to give us the opportunity to respond to the gospel story. I once heard a Chinese girl begin her testimony by reviewing how she had wanted to attend a top-tier university in the United States, but she was not accepted. She ultimately ended up at a second-choice university, but there the friendships she made gave her the opportunity to hear and respond to the gospel. In her testimony, she praised God for being rejected by her first choice of university. By sharing this, she confronted her hearers with the fact that God is actively involved in their lives.

For those of us who were born into a Christian family and made decisions for Christ at an early age, it is easy to see how our parents' faith influenced our own. We may express thankfulness for being born into that family, knowing how difficult it might have been for us to have heard the gospel if our situation had been different. We must remember, however, that even though God has been working for generations through a family, each of us had a decision. God still orchestrated circumstances to reach out to each of us. Unfortunately, not all children born to Christian parents accept Christ for themselves.

Much of the world believes that one automatically follows the religion of one's parents. Inadvertently, for those of us who were born to Christian parents, we often reinforce the belief that we are "what we are" because we were born into a family of that faith. When we begin our testimonies, "I was born into a Christian family…" it is possible the person to whom we are speaking is thinking of his or her parents and the fact that they are Muslim, or Hindu, or Humanists. When sharing our salvation testimony, we must carefully consider our words so that we do not reinforce this false belief.

If we have been Christians for a long time, we may be unaware of the "insider" language we use when we talk about our faith. As you have learned in our discussion of cognitive schemata, knowing the name of something implies that we know the "story" behind that item. In a group of Christian friends, I can say, "I'm always late for Sunday School," and they understand me because they have a schema for Sunday School. As a Christian, we have a developed vocabulary with words such as "salvation," "church," and "Christian." It is imperative that we understand what those words mean to others before we use them.

One of the first things my husband and I did when we moved to our Muslim village was ask the people what the word "Christian" meant to them. We received various replies. "An ethnic group in the south…a drunkard…someone who worships idols…someone who never prays, though if they do pray, they have to go in a building, and it is only once a week." When we asked who Jesus was, almost all said He was a great man and a prophet, though one man scratched his head and said questioningly, "Isn't He that guy in the movie?" We knew from the responses that we had to use language to describe our faith that the people would understand. Since they had such a negative connotation of Christians, we called ourselves "followers of Jesus." Once, an older woman who was visiting said boldly, "Other people said you are a Christian, but I told them that can't be true because you are too nice." Her remarks gave me an opportunity to talk about my faith and what it really means to be a Christian.

Because U.S. short-term partners often have not had the opportunity to share their salvation testimonies with people of other cultures, I sometimes asked them to write their testimonies to send to me before they arrived so that I could make suggestions on ways to limit "insider" language. The language they use may not only be "church" language but also reflect U.S. American cultural concepts that are difficult to translate. Sometimes, when people hear an unfamiliar concept, they spend time thinking about that instead of the actual message of the testimony. Not only is it important to limit vocabulary that is difficult to translate or understand, it is also important to include in our testimonies parts of the gospel message that will speak to the listeners. Here are two examples of testimonies from short-term partners that I adapted to meet the needs of our people. I have changed some of the details and the names. What the partner wrote is printed first. My suggested adaptation is in italics.

Testimony of a girl raised in a non-Christian home

I grew up in a non-Christian home with an abusive mother and loving father who traveled. My parents did not go to church, although they both had when they were growing up. My mother grew up in an abusive home, and then lived in a convent. My father grew up in an interdenominational church but quit going to church when he left home.

I grew up in a home where my mother did not take care of me like she should. My mother had been mistreated when she was a child, and she mistreated me. My father loved me but he often traveled. My parents did not know Jesus or know that God cares about them.

I periodically went to church with my best friend, Roberta Joiner, and her family who were neighbors of ours. I was keenly aware that their home was very different than mine. I loved spending time with the Joiner's. There was a peace in their home that I did not experience at my home, and I would try to spend as much time over there as possible.

I sometimes went to worship God with my best friend, Roberta, and her family who were our neighbors. Their family was very different than mine. I loved spending time in their courtyard. There was a peace in their family that I did not have in my family. I would try to stay in their courtyard as much as I could.

I remember going to Sunday School and learning about Jesus, who He was and what He did for me. I remember going to "big church" and loving the music. But most of all, I remember eating lunch on Sundays with the Joiner's. After dinner, they would have a family devotion and read from a little book and talk about what it meant. I had such a desire to have that home environment. I didn't recognize it at the time, but I had such a desire to know God and the peace that comes with Him.

I remember going with them to a place where we studied God's Word and learned about Jesus – who He was and what he did for me. I learned that God is holy and just, that He loves all people and wants to have a relationship with each person, man or woman. Because God is holy and just and because we are sinners, we need a sacrifice for our sins. I learned that long ago, Jesus came to earth. Jesus performed miracles. He raised people from death. He has power over Satan. Jesus died to give Himself as the sacrifice for our sins, so that we can know God. Jesus rose from death to show that He has power over death, just like God. We know that because of the miracles He did and because God's Word tells us, that Jesus was God who took the form of a man. God loves us that much. I learned that if we believe in Jesus and accept Him as the sacrifice for our sins, we become God's child forever. Nothing can separate us from God's love. Even death cannot separate us. I heard the story of God's love and how we can become God's child and have peace in our hearts by having faith in Jesus. The Joiners had that peace. I did not have that peace because I had not accepted Jesus as the sacrifice for my sins. I wanted to know more about how I could be like the Joiners and have peace in my heart.

In fifth grade, I asked my parents if they would come to church with me. My mom and I went to several catholic churches, but she was still very angry at "the church" (I didn't understand that then). Then my dad started going with us, although he would not go to a catholic church, so we started visiting protestant churches. The summer between 5th and 6th grade, I joined the church. During a youth retreat, I became a Christian. I knew I needed a Savior. I felt instantly that I was "home". I had such a desire to have peace in my life and to hold onto the Truth that God had a plan that intimately included me! I was baptized at the end of that summer. I stayed very involved in church through high school. Although my focus swayed from Christ to self, He always remained faithful to me.

I learned a lot about Jesus. One day, I decided I was tired of not having peace and decided to ask Jesus to be the sacrifice for my sins. I asked Jesus to forgive me for the wrong things I had done and for not believing in Him. I told God that I believed in Jesus and wanted to become God's child. I felt instantly that I was "home." I had a new family. I was part of God's family. From that time until today, I have peace in my heart and I know that God loves me. I was baptized to show others that my life had changed. I had friends who also followed Jesus. On Sundays, I enjoyed going to a gathering where we worshipped Jesus and talked about what he means to us. I have to admit, sometimes I did things I shouldn't do and did not pray or talk to Jesus like I should. Jesus did not abandon me. He always loved me, and waited for me to realize how much I needed Him.

My senior year of college, I realized that I was not living the life that God intended for me, and I didn't have my life grounded in Christ. I re-dedicated my life to live for Christ. Although I knew Jesus as my Savior, it was the first time I allowed Him to be the Lord of my Life. As I continue to grow closer to God, I realize that the peace I have in my life now only comes from knowing Him.

There was a time in my life, however, when I knew I was not doing the things God wanted me to do. I did things because I wanted to. I was not listening to God or asking God before I made decisions. Although I knew that Jesus was my Savior, I knew I needed to follow God in all areas of my life. Each day, as I trust God and learn more about Him, I realize that the peace I have in my life comes from knowing Him.

(My dad became a Christian when I was in the seventh grade. I am still praying for my mom.)

My dad also decided to follow Jesus, but my mother does not. I still pray that one day my mother will accept Jesus as her Savior. Would you like to know more about how you can have peace like mine?

Woman whose husband does not believe

I live in a home as a Christian woman with a husband who does not appear to have a close relationship with God. I say this because of his actions, lifestyle and by what I experience.

There was a time in my life when someone told me that I could have peace in my heart and a personal relationship with God if I accepted Jesus as the sacrifice for my sins and lived for him. I decided to follow Jesus, and I have much peace in my heart.

My husband does not follow Jesus like I do, however. I know that I, as a woman, was created in God's image. One day, after I die, I know that I will stand alone before God at the judgment. My husband, when he dies, will stand alone also. Even though my husband does not follow God like he should, when I stand before God at the judgment, I want God to be pleased with me.

He does not like it when I go to church for choir practice, for worship or for any additional church-related activity. He makes negative comments to me for going to church for different things. On Sundays, when I'm getting my children up to go to church they often say, "Why can't I stay home like Daddy? Or, "Why do we have to go every Sunday?" [My husband will come to church, but he is always late for the last service]. He feels that Sundays are a day of rest for him.

My husband does not like it when I go to worship God with other people who follow Jesus and usually says things to me to let me know he does not like it when I go. I worship with other believers on Sunday, and on Sunday mornings when I get my children ready to go to worship with me, they say to me, "Why can't I stay home like Daddy?" or "Why do we have to go worship every Sunday?" Sometimes my husband will come to worship but he is always late. He would rather sleep.

My husband often will not speak to me when I return from church. Sometimes, this can go on for at least a couple of days. He gives me the cold shoulder. He has said very hurtful things to me.

Sometimes when I get home from being with other people who believe in Jesus, my husband will not look at me or speak to me. Sometimes he does not speak to me for several days. Sometimes he says mean things to me.

It is only by the grace of God and from the encouragement of other Christian women that I am able to be encouraged. I believe that God can change my husband's heart, and I pray that He will. I know that God knows my situation, and I know that He hears and answers my prayers. I am able to have strength to love and respect my husband as my husband only because of who I am in Christ.

It is only through God's love and the care of other women believers who encourage me that I am able to remain at peace. I believe that God can change my husband's heart so that he will want to follow Jesus like I follow Jesus. I know that God knows everything about me, and He hears and answers my prayers. I pray for my husband, that one day, he too will want to follow Jesus. I am able to have the strength to love and respect my husband only because I know I have become God's child because of my faith in Jesus.

I pray without ceasing, fast and meditate on God's word such as 1 Peter 4:12-13. I cling to verses like Psalms 138:8, Psalms 34:18-19 and numerous others.

I pray all of the time. I fast and think about God's Word. These verses in God's Word are comforting to me. God's Word says, "When the fiery ordeal arises among you to test you, don't be surprised by it, as if something unusual were happening to you. Instead, as you share in the sufferings of the Messiah rejoice, so that you may also rejoice with great joy at the revelation of His glory. If you are ridiculed for the name of Christ, you are blessed, because the Spirit of glory and of God rests on you." In another place, God's Word says, "The Lord will fulfill His purpose for me. Lord, your love is eternal." It also says, "The Lord is near the brokenhearted; He saves those crushed in spirit. Many adversities come to the one who is righteous, but the Lord delivers him from them all."

Would you like to have peace in your heart like I have found peace? The only way is through accepting Jesus as the sacrifice for your sins. Would you like to hear more about how you can do this?

As you read through these testimonies and my suggested adaptations, did you notice some themes? I accepted Christ when I was six-years-old. Though I am glad that God was working in my heart at that young age, I have learned that when I begin my testimony by telling my age, people's thoughts begin to wander. They fixate on my age rather than on the message of my testimony. I have learned to say, "There was a time in my life…"

As you have learned, our testimonies should include what our lives were like before Christ when we discovered we had need of Him, what happened - the process of accepting Christ, and what our life is like now that we believe. Stories of how God works in our life are our faith stories. Though we have one salvation story, we should all have many, many faith stories. If we do not, it is because we have not opened our eyes. Though it is important to be able to share our salvation story, sharing our faith stories not only encourages others, it can encourage us as well. We all have "markers" in our lives where God worked miraculously. These are stories we love to share. We should not only share these "markers" but current faith stories as well. We should have a new faith story to share at least weekly.

Faith Stories

Some may believe that unless their stories illustrate our U.S. American value of "success," that they do not have a faith story. We all love the stories of hundreds of converts and churches planting churches. We love the stories of successful, love-filled marriages and obedient children who grow up to make wise decisions. We are hesitant to share the stories of disillusionment, conflict, and struggle, however. How, we may think, can it help someone else to admit our weaknesses or even our failures? We forget the doubts depicted in the Psalms, the New Testament portraits of Christians making poor decisions. When we hide behind our masks, those to whom we are witnessing get the wrong impression. They may believe that if they accept Christ their lives will be perfect like ours and then become disillusioned when they accept Christ but their struggles continue. Too many times, I am afraid our message is heard as one of God's provision instead of God's decision to leave the thorns in our flesh. Three women in a U.S. short-term partnership group that were to assist with an African women's meeting in one of our churches each told me the same thing, "I do not know why I am here." Each woman had recently undergone a major difficulty in her life and were present only because others in their church had paid for their trips. One woman had witnessed the business she operated with her husband go bankrupt. One had seen her husband, a leader in their church, walk away from their long marriage to be with the younger woman with whom he was having an affair. One had been dealing with an adult son who was a drug addict. The women knew God wanted them on the mission trip, but they each were concerned because they had "nothing to share." I told them that I knew exactly why God wanted them on the trip as I pointed out how God had given them the grace to go through their difficulties. I asked that they be open and honest at the women's meeting by giving their testimonies of the difficulties they had undergone, were undergoing, and how they saw God's faithfulness. They reluctantly agreed. They were concerned because they saw their situations as failures rather than the successes about which we love to talk.

The women's meeting began with the usual songs and devotion. The African women sat on one side of the building, eyeing the American women on the other. Everyone was on her best, church-like, behavior. Then, one by one, the American women shared as I translated their testimonies. The Spirit moved as the African women were touched by the heartfelt testimonies. By hearing the testimonies of the American women, it was as if a flood-gate opened. The African women began to share similar happenings in their own lives – unemployment, marriage issues, heartbreak because of children who had made poor decisions. The African woman also reached out to the short-term partners, promising to pray for them, showing their love. There were many tears that day as everyone, the American and African women alike, were reminded of God's faithfulness in the midst of difficulty. Cultural barriers fell. We were sisters in Christ.

We each have faith stories of how we see God at work in the world around us. How is God working in your life? Do you see him working? When you see Him, do you just accept His provision, or do you testify about it?

Our faith story is a chronicle of our journey with God. There are three major components involved in sharing faith stories. We must first recognize when and where God is working in our lives, past and present. Second, we must look to God's Word to see if there are passages or biblical stories that correspond to our circumstances. When we share our faith stories, we should also look for ways to share God's Word. Third, we must not only share our faith stories with others who believe as we do, we must also intentionally share our faith stories with unbelievers.

How easy life would be if God would give us a map with all of our major decisions marked and an arrow showing us which way to turn. If only all of the pitfalls were circled in red so we could choose an alternate route. In my life, I have found the hardest decisions are not necessarily those between good and bad but those between better and best. When my husband and I felt it was time to look for a new place of service after planting multiple churches in one location, it was not easy to decide where to move. We informed leadership of our desire to change locations, and they agreed that it was time for us to move on. Though we considered, and visited, multiple places in our area, we did not feel a clear leading one way or the other. A mature colleague told me, "I have found that sometimes God leads from behind. You have to make a decision. If it is the wrong one, He will let you know." She was right. We decided, and He let us know. We believed that we needed to go to the capital city of another country to do urban evangelism and confidently announced our decision to leadership. The leader of our region told us that the leadership team had met recently, and they would prefer if we moved to a remote village in another country to work among a strategic unreached people group. We were shocked. That people group had not even been on our radar. Our leader asked us to pray about the decision. We were told the ultimate decision was ours. After a few days of prayer and discussion, we decided that though we had been excited about our original plan and still felt it was the way we should go, we had to respect authority. If leadership felt we needed to be in the village, we needed to trust them. We chose to go to the village, though my heart was not totally in the choice – at first. God worked miraculously. Over the next few months, He made it abundantly clear that He wanted us there. That is a faith story that I enjoy sharing, but it happened long ago.

Though in the midst of circumstances it may be difficult to see God's hand, in retrospect, it is often easy to see how God managed circumstances in our lives. Our faith stories are not only the account of how we have seen God working over time, however. They must also include what God is doing each week. Our faith stories should include fresh accounts of seeing God. A few days ago, a student came by my office on campus to ask me to review a paper he had written for a religion class. As a graduate student, my job was to help newer students adjust to academic life. I had not seen this particular student in four months. His assignment was to visit a church service of a denomination different from his own and to write about the experience. From his paper, it was obvious he was not a Christian. When we reviewed his paper, I not only talked about the grammar and content, I also shared the gospel. When he left my office, he said he had a lot to think about. This young man's visit was a reminder of how God orchestrates circumstances, bringing people to Himself. It made me smile.

When we are conscious of how God is working and want to share that with others, we should look for biblical passages or stories that correspond to our faith story. By telling my faith story of how God led us to our village, I can use that opportunity to tell the story of God calling Abraham. Just as God asked Abraham to leave his home and was not specific about Abraham's future, so we knew that God wanted us to leave but were unsure of the destination. Abraham obeyed, and God worked through him. We knew, like Abraham, that we needed to be obedient. Unlike Abraham, we had Christian leadership who helped point the way. In the next chapters, we will learn more about sharing Bible stories as we witness. If we know biblical stories that correspond to a contemporary situation, it should become natural to insert the Bible story after sharing our faith story. We then point listeners to the Bible and help them see the importance of God's Word to our daily lives.

For those of us who have been Christians for a long time, we may become used to seeing God working in our lives. When we become aware of God's hand, we may even hold that experience close to our heart, anxious to share it the next time we are with Christian friends. Why do we think we must wait? Though it may seem natural to talk about God's provision or intervention when sharing with Christian friends who believe as we do, are we telling these same faith stories in intentional evangelism? We must not forget to brag on God, to tell others about our active, personal, relationship with Him. We must not only tell stories of God's provision but also stories of God's conviction, of the times when His grace was sufficient. Much of the world has no idea such a relationship can exist. Soon after I began the doctoral program, I became aware of which professors and which students had a glowing relationship with Christ and who did not. As I thought about how I could witness, I knew that how I approached my coursework would speak volumes to the professors and my classmates about not only who I am but also who Christ is. The advice for writers of fiction (showing is stronger than telling) also applies, in part, to our witness. In many circumstances, we must earn the right to tell by showing. However, showing and never telling may lead others to think that the power they see in our lives originates with us alone. As my doctoral studies drew to a close, professors and classmates were more attentive to my telling because of my reputation as a serious student. We should always be ready not only to share stories from God's Word but also to share the hope that is within us.

"I was worried," Stacey said. "This is the first time his fever has been so high." Stacey ran her hand over Bryan's fuzzy head cradled against her chest. Conscious that Mark was asleep in their bedroom, she spoke through the screen door to Muhammad as he waited outside.

"He looks fine to me." Muhammad said. Stacey nodded.

"We were up most of the night. I just rocked him and prayed, rocked and prayed. His fever broke early this morning. Mark didn't get much sleep. He was worried, too. I can go wake him if you want. He would probably want me to."

"Don't worry about it. I can come back this afternoon when my shift at the radio station is over. Mark is making a lot of progress."

"Yes," Stacey said. "It is very difficult on him that he cannot share everything in his heart." Muhammad nodded as he turned to leave.

"Muhammad?" Stacey asked. Muhammad turned back toward her, raising his eyebrow.

"Yes?" he answered. Stacey pushed open the door and went to stand beside Muhammad in their courtyard, careful of the sleeping baby in her arms.

"Have you ever wondered why Mark and I are living here, why we left our family, why we took Bryan away from his grandparents?" Muhammad shrugged his shoulders.

"I'm just glad you're here," he said.

"I will be honest," Stacey said. "It is hard being away from my parents. The first thing I did last night when Bryan was so sick was call them and ask them to pray. We're here because God told us to come here." Muhammad looked at her quizzically. "We're here because we have a relationship with God. When we were worried last night, Mark and I prayed. We felt God's presence. Yes," she said as she put the back of her hand against Bryan's forehead, relieved at the coolness. "God answered our prayers and Bryan is better. But even if Bryan had gotten worse, we knew that we were not alone. We came here to show the people how they, too, can have that kind of relationship with God." Muhammad nodded slowly.

"That is all that Mark talks about now" he said.

"I had to say something," Stacey added. "There are many stories in the Bible where the sick came to Jesus and He healed them. Jesus even healed a man who was born blind. Those people were overjoyed and thankful, just like I am thankful this morning." Stacey bent down to kiss the top of Bryan's head, careful not to wake him. "My heart is so full. I just had to say something. I wanted you to know that God deserves our praise."

"I understand," Muhammad said as he turned. "You sound like Marie. I used to think that Christians never pray. But, Marie prays all the time. More than me," he added sheepishly before heading down the path and out into the sunshine.

Part III

Sharing Stories with the World

CHAPTER 7

God's Word in Our Hearts

Mark grabbed his local language Bible from the shelf as he saw Muhammad approaching. For several months, they had begun their sessions with Mark reading passages from the Bible while Muhammad corrected his pronunciation. It was nice to have a Bible available in the local language, even if it were slightly different from their dialect and most of the people in the village did not know how to read. In the beginning, Mark had read random verses, but at their supervisor John's suggestion, Mark had begun reading stories from a list that John had given him. Mark had even begun to take the Bible with him on his walks with Muhammad, telling the men who played cards at the store that he wanted them to correct his pronunciation. He could tell they were becoming interested in the stories he read. The day before, he had purposively left his Bible at home, anxious to see how the men would react. They had been disappointed.

Muhammad entered and the two men shook hands and went through the ritualistic greetings. "Stacey had to go to the market," Mark said. "She should be back soon.

Muhammad saw the Bible in Mark's hand. "Are you going to read?"

"Actually," replied Mark. "I thought we could try something different. Today, instead of reading, I want to tell the story."

"Why?" asked Muhammad.

"Because I won't always have the Bible with me or be able to read. I need some exercise, and I asked Henri if I could go with him to help him weed his fields. If I learn the story, I can tell it to him while we are hoeing."

Muhammad narrowed his eyes. "Work in the fields?" he said. "Are you sure you are up to that?"

"I'm stronger than I look." Mark added defensively. "Here," he said as he thrust the Bible into Muhammad's hands and pointed to a passage in Exodus. "You follow along to see if what I'm telling is accurate." Muhammad looked uncomfortable as he held the Bible in his hands. This is the first time he's held a Bible, Mark realized. His tone softened as he motioned for Muhammad to sit on the couch. "Do you mind doing this?" he asked.

"Not at all," Muhammad said. "Actually, I have enjoyed listening to you" he added quietly as he searched the page.

As Christians, we all have Scripture that we have hidden in our hearts be it verses we have memorized or stories we have learned. If we were suddenly put in a place where we had no access to the written Word and were told to write what we remembered, what would that Scripture look like?

When my husband and I taught Chronological Bible Storying (CBS) conferences to local pastors, I often asked what would happen if I held my camera close to their minds and took pictures of the Bibles there. When I developed the pictures, what would I see? We all smiled at the absurdity of the task, but they began to think. I would then ask, "And if I came to your church with my camera, and I walked up to the Chairman of the Deacons and took a picture of the Bible there and went to the older ladies in your congregation who do not read, what would I find? Would the Bible in their minds resemble in any way the written Word, or would it be a terrible jumble of verses, biblical stories, and sermon illustrations with no clear timeline or understanding of what belongs in the New Testament and what belongs in the Old Testament? Unless someone memorizes the entire Bible, it is obviously impossible to have a Bible in our minds.

There is a distinction between the whole written Bible and Scripture portions. According to Wycliffe Bible Translators, 1.3 billion people do not have the full Bible translated into their first language. They may have the New Testament, one book of the Bible, or Scripture portions, but they do not have the full Bible.

For those of us who do have the full Bible translated into our language and we can read, we have a choice. If we do not hide God's Word in our hearts, we can always pick up the Bible itself and find the verse we want. However, for those who cannot read or those who do not have the full Bible translated into their language, it is probable that the only Bible to which they have access is the one that they can recall. Yes, perhaps they can listen to a recorded Bible, if such a recording exists, and they have the equipment to listen to it. Perhaps, someone who is literate in their social network will read the Bible to them, if it has been translated into their language and the literate has time. Perhaps, they will hear portions of the Bible if they attend church. Perhaps...

Even with these possibilities, without learning Bible stories and having a basic understanding of where those stories fall in a biblical timeline, it is unlikely the Scriptures nonliterates carry in their minds resemble the Holy Scripture. If they have heard sermons that contained isolated verses, contemporary illustrations, or parts of stories, how do they know what belongs in God's Word and what does not? Hearing someone say, "John 3:16 is my favorite verse," has no meaning.

In this final part, we will discuss the importance of sharing stories from God's Word with the world. Though it is impossible to give nonliterates a full Bible, we can help them organize the Scriptures they learn so that those Scriptures follow a biblical timeline and are easier to recall. We can help them hide God's Word in their hearts so that they can carry it anywhere.

God's Word convicts and instructs, whether it is Scripture we have hidden in our hearts or words we read on a printed page. When Jesus encountered the men on the road to Emmaus, He made use of their knowledge of the Scriptures. Beginning with Moses and the Prophets, Jesus "interpreted for them the things concerning Himself in all the Scriptures" (Luke 24:27b). The Scriptures Jesus used to teach the men originated with the written Word but it was not the written Word that Jesus used that day. Jesus taught the men using the Scriptures they had in their hearts.

Learning a Story from the Bible

When the Bible is available in our language in multiple translations, as it is in English, we should rely on the written text as we learn the story. Some choose to memorize the verses of the story from a familiar translation. Rote memorization involves the ability to recall information exactly as it was given. This information can be isolated and does not necessarily have to be understood to be repeated. Memorizing an entire story can prove difficult and may inhibit someone from sharing the story with others for fear of forgetting part of the story.

Instead of choosing a translation and memorizing the entire story, one can work from the text to memorize the story framework. To determine the story framework, we need to determine the main characters and the story events. It is important to know what is and what is not in the story. Though we are free to streamline the story and leave out details, we are not free to add details or characters to the story. Larger stories that encompass multiple events in characters' lives may need to be broken into smaller stories that comprise one or two events or life stages.

Outlining a text, discovering the theme and sequence of main events, is a skill that is taught at an early age in U.S. American schools. In other school systems, this skill may not be taught until high school. When teaching storying conferences in Africa, I found it helpful to model the skill of discovering a sequence of events from a story or written text. I began by telling a brief story, just the facts, of a situation where thieves stole a truck from a missionary family. The story included the thieves taking the truck from the family, the ultimate capture of the thieves, and the recovery of the truck by police in a border town. I then told the same story a second time. The second time, I added more details. I then told the same story a third time, adding many more details as well as conversations between characters. Following my telling of the third story, I asked the participants, "Which of the three stories was true?" When the participants responded that all three of the stories were true, I asked which story was the most interesting and which would be the easiest to repeat. They admitted that the story with the fewest details would be the easiest to repeat, but the story with the most details was the most interesting.

In my modeling, I repeated the exercise with a biblical story. I asked someone to read a story, often The Tower of Babel, and together we listed the characters and main events from the story on the board. At that point, the participants saw how they could choose to include or leave out details but there was always a story structure which included main characters and a sequence of events. I asked several of them to tell the story from the events. Though some could do this, often they found that while telling the story, they would include a detail that was not in the list of main events. Unsure, they needed to check the written story text in the Bible to be sure their telling was accurate. As literates, even when we memorize the events, as we practice telling the story, it is not unusual to go back and forth between telling the story and searching the biblical text because we want to be sure what we are saying is accurate.

The first steps in memorizing a story when a written biblical text is available is:

1. Read the story in its entirety.

2. Determine if the story is a larger story or needs to be broken into sub-stories with fewer characters or events.

3. Once the story is chosen, identify the characters.

4. Outline the main events in the story.

5. Memorize the main events in order.

6. Tell the story from the main events, checking the Bible for accuracy as needed.

In following these steps, we have the story framework and may be able to recite a story. Learning a story from God's Word goes beyond being able to recite it, however. Being able to recite a story does not mean that we have hidden the story in our hearts. Learning includes understanding not only the single story but also where it fits in the broader story. Learning a story involves making it a part of us. We learn a story through repetition, by telling it, and by reading the story in multiple English translations and in other languages that we know. Because I speak French, reading a story in the French Bible sometimes gives me additional insight into the story.

Learning implies we have gone beyond external memory cues such as notes or pictures. In discussing the use of pictures as a memory aid, Paul Koehler in his book *Telling God's Story with Power*, explained that when he and his wife first trained storytellers Koehler gave them a book of pictures to show when sharing the stories. Koehler became concerned that the storytellers were relying on the pictures to remind them of elements in the story rather than internalizing the stories. This concern was proven correct when monsoon rains destroyed some of the books, and the storytellers were not confident in their abilities to tell the stories without the pictures. When training local believers to tell biblical stories, Koehler recommended using a symbol for each story to aid their memory instead of pictures.

When we have learned a story, we can tell it with minimal detail, average detail, and maximum detail. Every detail we include can be found in a written account of the story in a Bible. No details are included that are not present in a written biblical account. When we no longer have to check a written text to see if we are telling the story correctly, when we can tell the story in multiple situations, in multiple time frames, then the story is learned.

When we know that we will be asked to share a story that we have not told in a while, as literates, many of us read the story text in the Bible during our preparation. Because we are used to having stored information in writing instead of relying on our memories, reading the text to ourselves as we prepare can give us confidence because it confirms our knowledge. This revision is especially important when we are between the memorizing and learning stage.

When our audience does not have a written Bible available to them, we begin with our own written text and put the story into their language. In putting the story in another language, we or someone we trust needs to be familiar with that language. Word for word translation usually does not work. There is a good reason why translation projects usually take years as the translators uncover the meanings behind words. From our discussion of cognitive schemata, you understand the layers of meaning that hover behind single words. Words in all languages have schemata of meaning attached to them. When a word in a particular language is part of common vocabulary, normally the word is used without the users stopping to engage in critical thinking. Translators have a difficult task, for rarely do word meanings and their corresponding schemata match perfectly from culture to culture. Some who have not heard of the gospel may not have words for concepts we think everyone understands.

Once when my husband and I were teaching storying to students in an African Bible school, we assigned various stories for the students to learn. One student, who was assigned the story of Jacob and Esau, raised his hand and said, "I don't think I should use this word here in the Bible that is used for "twins." When we asked for an explanation, he continued.

"The word here in the Bible is the word in our language for twins, but it is also the word for "genies," or conniving spirits." The director of the Bible School who was with us spoke that language and had preached from that passage many times.

"What?" he gasped, and rushed to look at the passage in the printed Bible. Soon, the other students in the class were hovered over the Bible. The Bible school director shook his head and said, "I've never noticed that before. In our culture, the people believe that twins are really genies come to earth. We have no other word for 'twins.' I guess when the Bible was translated, the translators used that word because there is no other word." I could not help but think of the many times pastors had preached on that passage or Christians had read that Rebekah gave birth to genies, conniving spirits. We discussed the issue, then agreed that the student should not use the local word for twins, but say, "Rebekah gave birth to two babies at the same time" (Genesis 25:24). The Bible school director, embarrassed at the error, promised to speak to the local Bible society to ask that the problem be addressed before subsequent printings.

As this example shows, translation difficulties can occur when those involved are Christians. We must be careful especially when translators are not believers. My husband and I already spoke the local language when we moved to our village. Because there were some dialectical differences, we asked a local man to help us translate some verses. We already had the printed Bible in a language that was very close to the language of our village. We asked, "How do you say, 'God is love?'" We knew there were several words in the language for love and wanted to know which word he would use. He thought for a moment, then replied literally,

"God gives us food." We knew that was incorrect, and tried, unsuccessfully, to have him translate what we had said. He insisted his translation was correct. We knew the way to show "essence" in the language. When we said "God is love" using that form, basically saying that the essence of God is love, he would not accept what we said. I do not believe that we were grammatically incorrect. However, as a Muslim, the concept of God's essence being love is far removed from his belief system. It was so far removed that he could not bring himself to verbalize it. I knew what he was telling me was incorrect because I already knew the language. If one does not already know the language, a translation needs to be back-translated multiple times with multiple people to be certain the terminology used agrees with biblical truth.

In order to be certain we are communicating accurate meanings, terms such as "God," "Holy Spirit," "sin," "eternal life," "love," and others need to be discussed. There may not be a word in the language corresponding to these concepts. If there is a team of Bible translators working in the language, it is a good idea to ask for their help. Though we are anxious to have stories we can begin sharing and we do not want to wait the years it may take for Bible translations, we must not take lightly the responsibility of having an accurate translation of a story. When we are telling the story in English and using a translator, we must be certain that the translator is using the correct terminology. If we say, "God is love," and the translator tells the people, "God gives us food," we are not communicating as we would like. When short-term partnership teams traveled to villages to witness through translators, we found it helpful if the team were accompanied by a mature African Christian who spoke the language. Even if that Christian could not speak English, he or she could listen to the translators and correct any misinformation.

As was discussed in Chapter Six, we should avoid using words in our salvation stories or personal faith stories that reflect our culture and do not correspond to a concept in the listener's language. We also need to be careful that the words we use in our stories communicate. Christians communicate with each other because they share schemata, meanings. Unbelievers, whether they are neighbors, co-workers, or people from a different language and culture, do not share a Christian schema. Even as a believer, the more I experience God, the more my schema of God grows. Our hearers are probably not familiar with the biblical context. A description of the context is needed when sharing the Bible with the unchurched be they in the United States or elsewhere.

When developing a story to tell to a nonliterate, I am always conscious that we are living in an increasingly literate world. It may be that the person with whom I am sharing the story is not literate and does not have access to a printed Bible. However, the Bible has been translated into the major world languages. New literacy studies is an emerging research field that looks at how nonliterates have access to literacy through someone in their social network who is literate. The nonliterates may be comfortable in orality but because their children go to school or they have to interact with government health clinics, they are aware of literacy. When these nonliterates need something read or written, they ask for help from someone who is literate. It is therefore conceivable that the person with whom I am sharing the story may hear the story read at some time or ask a literate friend to translate it from the written Word. If the person hears the story read someday, I want the reading to confirm the story I have shared.

The Spiritual Discipline of Learning Stories

We are familiar with the spiritual disciplines of personal Bible study and prayer. What does your Bible study look like? Do you follow a devotional guide, a workbook, a calendar of Bible readings that ensures you will read the entire Bible in a year? Though memorizing Scripture may be a part of your study, have you considered learning Bible stories? As has been discussed, hiding God's Word in our hearts is not limited to Scripture memorization. Sometimes, when we encourage people to learn Bible stories it appears as if the reason we are encouraging people to learn stories is to equip them to tell the stories. The emphasis is on others hearing the gospel in a way they can understand. Probably what needs to be stressed more, however, is that learning a Bible story allows us to have a fresh encounter with Scriptures. Learning a story means we move from learning about God's Word to learning God's Word. Below are six reasons why learning Bible stories should be a part of our devotional lives.

Learning a Bible Story Forces Us to Get Serious with God's Word. Too often, in our busy schedules, personal Bible "study" is limited to reading a few verses someone else has suggested in a devotional guide or working through a study book that someone else has written. In our specialist mentality, we may think we do not have the knowledge or the resources to actually study the Scriptures for ourselves. In learning a Bible story, we must first select which story we are going to learn, from which passage. We search the Bible. We move from reading a passage to reading a passage for the purpose of telling it.

Learning a Bible Story Gives Us a Fresh Perspective on God's Word. When we have selected the story, we think about the characters and the major events. As we work to memorize the story, we tend to notice verses that we had read previously, but never thought about. When learning the story of Jesus Walking on the Water following the feeding of the 5,000 in Matthew 14:22-33, I noticed in verse 22 that Jesus made the disciples get in the boat and sent them away before Jesus Himself dismissed the crowds. Would it not have been easier if the disciples had helped Him with that chore? Surely, after being fed, the crowds would not want to disburse? What tone did Jesus use? Were the disciples giddy from witnessing the miracle? Did Jesus send them away because He needed some down time from them as much as He needed the crowds to leave? We cannot know the answers to these questions, but these questions did not surface until I read the passage with the intent on learning it in order to be able to tell it.

Learning a Bible Story Gives Us Insight. In using the same example of learning the story of Jesus Walking on the Water, I noticed that prior to that event was the beheading of John the Baptist. Scripture says that when Jesus heard the news, He tried to withdraw but because of the needs of the crowd, He had compassion on them and taught them. Ultimately, He fed at least 5,000. Jesus then put the disciples in the boat, sent the crowds away, and went up a mountain to pray. When evening came, He was finally alone. As I contemplated this story, I realized that Jesus, because of His compassion, had postponed His grieving. The whole time He had taught and even performed the miracle, His heart must have been breaking because of the cruel way in which His cousin had died. I realized that like Jesus, sometimes we must get on with the process of living and serving others, even when we are grieving.

Learning a Bible Story Brings Us Into the Story. A written text is outside of ourselves. It invites reflection. With the written Word, we can easily contemplate a text because it is fixed and separate from ourselves. When we learn a story to tell it, however, speech brings a certain immediacy to the writing as the text is brought to life. In speech, we are conscious of tone, inflection, emphasis, and pauses. Each of these qualities of speech carries meaning. In the passage of Jesus Walking on the Water, when Jesus says to Peter, "Why did you doubt?" I have a choice. When I ask that question, I can use a quizzical, caring, or disciplinary tone. I can choose which word to emphasize. "WHY did you doubt?" has a slightly different meaning than "Why did YOU doubt?" Deciding on how I will speak these words draws me into the story. I am no longer only an observer but a participant in sharing meaning.

Learning a Bible Story Equips Us if God Wants to Use Us. At one of our storying courses in Africa, students learned the story from Genesis 2 of the Creation of the First Man and Woman. Several days later, a pastor who was a member of the class related how he had been visiting family and the husband and wife kept arguing during his visit. He said God brought the story he had learned to mind, and he told the husband and wife to stop arguing because they were both made in God's image and needed to care about each other. He then told them the story of the Creation of the First Man and Woman. He said the husband and wife were convicted that they were not treating each other properly and stopped arguing. The pastor said the couple easily accepted him telling them the story but he did not think they would have been as agreeable had he taken his Bible and read them the passage. Knowing the story equipped him to be used by God. I believe that once we take the step to learn a story from God's Word, God will give us an opportunity either to share with others what we are learning from the experience or to tell the story to those who need to hear it.

Learning a Bible Story Promotes Our Spiritual Growth. It is not easy to learn a Bible story. We literates are not used to exercising our memories. Learning a Bible story takes discipline as we struggle with the story, the characters, and the meaning. As we internalize the story, however, we follow the commandment to hide God's Word in our hearts.

This chapter began with the question of what would happen if we were placed in a situation where we had no access to the written Word and had to write down the Scripture that was in our minds. I asked, what would that Scripture look like? In today's world, this scenario may not be as strange as it sounds. If you were imprisoned for your faith, would the isolated verses you have memorized be enough to encourage you and others? Would you be able to share stories from God's Word? After growing up in Sunday School, we may think we know the Bible stories. I challenge you. Without looking at the Scripture, tell the story of Jesus Walking on the Water as it is portrayed in Matthew. Tell it to yourself in the mirror, then check the passage to see if you were correct. Knowing about God's Word and knowing God's Word is not the same.

"It isn't that I don't know how to read," explained Marie. "I just don't have time." She was standing over the boiling pot balanced securely on the small open fire. "With hauling water, cooking, selling bananas at the market, and taking care of Anna..." At that moment, cries from the direction of the mat where Anna had been sleeping caught the women's attention.

"Give me that," Stacey said, taking the long wooden stirring paddle from Marie's hand. "I can stir until you get her." Marie headed toward Anna, effortlessly swung the baby onto her back, wrapped a cloth around her, and headed back to the fire. "Since Bryan is with Mark, I won't be distracted," Stacey said. "What I would like to do is work with you to learn Bible stories. I can read the story from the Bible, and we can discuss it. Then, I will tell it to you, and you can correct my grammar. You can tell it to me, and I can see if I understand you."

"That's a wonderful idea," said Marie. "My aunt is at home now, but she has never regained her strength after her illness. She just lies in bed all day. We can visit her and tell her the stories, too. She isn't a Christian and she doesn't like it when I talk about my faith, but I think she would be willing to listen to a story.

"That is a good idea. I think this will help both of us. I am so glad we can communicate now and talk about God's Word."

"Yes, Muhammad is a good teacher," Marie said proudly.

CHAPTER 8

Listening, Telling, and Sharing

Mark watched the flies as they landed and took off from the hairs on his forearm. He knew better than to swat them for that would just make them angry and they would swirl around his lips. Still… enough was enough… His lower body was growing numb from being sandwiched between the men on the bench. They had been working in the fields all day. It was hot. He tried not to wrinkle his nose. He would have been a lot more comfortable in shorts and a muscle shirt, but Muhammad had warned him that that attire was only appropriate when he played soccer. He tried to play soccer with the boys from the village whenever he could. Mark reached down and fanned his long robe, tempted to pull it up to catch a breeze. After all, he was wearing shorts underneath. The men were once again shuffling the cards as one of Mark's neighbors stood up to leave. Mark quickly scooted over. Finally, he could breathe. He looked up to catch the glint of amusement in Muhammad's eyes from where he leaned comfortably against a tree. The men always insisted that Mark have the place of honor on the bench. He would rather have been under the tree with Muhammad where there was at least a breeze. One of the men dealing the cards started talking about a cow that had wandered into his field and eaten some of the corn. Mark had already heard the story. Five times. Mark stood up and reached for his Bible that he had wrapped in a cloth and placed on a shelf before he sat down. He had learned the hard way not to put it on the ground or on the bench beside him for the men respected the book, even if they did not understand its contents. He would read a few verses from the story first, then tell it. The men seemed to like the reading. At least they respected Bible. Mark laughed at the appropriate place when the man once again demonstrated how he had chased the cow from the cornfield. Mark looked at Muhammad who nodded slightly. "Would you like me to read you a story?" he said to the men around him. He opened to the passage and had just started to read when a teenage boy approached and asked the store proprietor for matches. Mark closed the Bible as Muhammad's cousin Ali stood, stretched, and headed inside to search for matches. A few minutes later, Ali returned and seated himself at the makeshift card table. Again, Mark opened the Bible. This time he began reading as the men continued playing cards, listening intently.

Communication Models and Discipleship

In Part I, we discussed different communication styles. We learned that the transmission style of communication emphasizes the message that is transmitted between the messenger and the receiver. This style of communication is the prevalent communication style of U.S. Americans. In this style, the message's form and content as well as the chosen mode to transmit the message are of primary importance. We see the transmission communication style used frequently today when a conversation does not have to be face-to-face but can take place rapidly through email or instant messaging.

It is easy to see how our communication style preference has impacted the way in which we disciple new converts. One of the first things I do when someone becomes a believer is get him or her a Bible. In the United States, that means going to the Christian bookstore, picking out an easy-to-read translation, and getting the person's name printed on the front in gold lettering. Add a basic discipleship book to give to the new convert along with the Bible and my responsibility is almost done. In Africa, I also worked to see that the new convert had access to God's Word. In my early ministry, because we had the Bible in the language, that meant teaching the person to read and encouraging the person to go to church to hear God's Word. In my later ministry, when I had been exposed to the needs of oral communicators, I worked to help oral communicators organize Scripture in their minds for easy recall using a method called Chronological Bible Storying (CBS). In this method, I shared and helped the listeners learn selected biblical stories that revealed truths they needed to understand in order to make an informed decision to accept Christ. The stories were presented in chronological order and were chosen not only because they contained necessary truths for salvation but also because the stories addressed barriers in the listeners' beliefs that might keep them from accepting Christ. In my discipleship efforts, the Bible, God's message to us, always takes primary importance, and rightly so. I want the new convert to have access to that message directly from the source. With the person's conversion, I saw my discipling responsibility as stepping out of the messenger role as quickly as possible and helping the person establish a relationship directly with the Source. Following the transmission method of communication, the messenger is God, the message is the Bible, and the new convert is the receiver.

In this communication model, we emphasize the message, God's Word. We use terms like "dig into," and we appreciate the insight of others who have taken the time to analyze words and phrases, consider the context, and pull out truths. We read God's Word ourselves and seek personal revelation and guidance. This communication model works well. A drawback, however, is that we may tend to see parts rather than the whole. We memorize verses, especially promises that make us feel better about a situation. We may not bother to read the paragraph or understand the context of the verse. We may not understand that the promise was made to a particular people at a particular time or that we do not have the right to appropriate the promise for ourselves. We may have head knowledge about God's Word but do not particularly understand how that Word applies practically to our daily lives. We expect our pastor to be trained to analyze and interpret Scripture and pay him to spend time delving into God's Word in order to share what he finds with us. We may expect "more" from those whom we pay to become specialists of God's Word. We depend on these analysts to share their findings.

At a graduate seminar once, I realized that many of the other attendees were graduate students from the Religion Department of the university. I listened as they discussed their dissertations and whether or not they agreed with one professor's interpretation of a verse they had discussed in class that morning. Following the seminar, I approached one of the students to express my willingness to speak to students in their department about how to witness to Muslim women. The student looked at me curiously then said, "I don't know of anyone interested in that topic. We're the Religion Department. You need to speak to someone in the seminary. Actually, you probably need to speak to someone in the missions department of the seminary. We just study the Bible." She crinkled her face for a moment as she spoke the words, so I knew she realized deep down that there was an issue with what she said. It appeared as if she saw those in her department as the "hearers" and if I wanted the "doers," I would need to go to the seminary missions department. She probably saw the surprise on my face, but turned quickly to her fellow students to fall back into their discussion of the meaning of a passage.

In the transaction communication model, communication takes place simultaneously between the messenger and the receiver as each sends and receives a message. The context is also part of the communication. The relationship between the messenger and receiver can be as important as the message. We see this communication model in apprenticeship and modeling. It is not only the information on how to do something that is transmitted but it is the experience, the body language, the "event" that is communicated. It may be difficult for us to understand how discipleship looks in the transaction model of communication.

When he was in his 70's, my father-in-law was approached by a fellow deacon and asked if he would like to be trained to do hospital visitation as a church ministry. The deacon was aging and wanted to pass along this ministry to someone else while he could. My father-in-law agreed. The deacon did not give my father-in-law a book. He did not schedule a meeting once a week to discuss the best ways to minister in the hospital. Instead, he said, "Follow me." For several months, my father-in-law went visiting with the deacon, observing while the other man took the lead. After each visit, they would discuss what had happened. My father-in-law soon began visiting on his own and felt confident continuing the ministry. He told me recently that by observing he learned not only what to do but what not to do. He felt his mentor sometimes stayed too long, overtiring the patients. When it was his turn to take over the ministry, he limited the time of his visits.

We see the command to use the transaction communication model in Scripture when Paul tells us to be imitators of God as dearly loved children (Ephesians 5:1). Paul also said to imitate him as he imitated Christ (1 Corinthians 11:1). Paul praised the believers in Thessalonica who imitated him (1 Thessalonians 1:6). We can learn to imitate God from understanding more about Him in His Word. We can discover what to do as well as what not to do when we study different biblical characters. The role models in my life, others who followed God, have also been great teachers as I learned through observing their lives.

Because I am very individualistic, complete with a love of personal privacy and a desire for "space," the transaction model of communication and discipleship are difficult for me. I have always been uncomfortable with Paul's "imitating me" emphasis. I know my humanity. I am conscious of my imperfections. It is easier to keep going to God and asking His forgiveness than straightening myself up in order to be ready for others to imitate. I do not think I am alone.

As mentioned previously, Jesus used both the transmission model and the transaction model of communication. He tended to use the transmission model with the crowds as He shared information with them. Even then, because they were mostly oral communicators, He used parables and stories to ensure that they received His message. With His disciples, He sometimes explained directly using the transmission model, but I believe His greatest impact was showing them how to live through the transaction model. Jesus was not only available to them, He used such opportunities to teach. It was not only the message that Jesus gave but the relationship He shared with His disciples.

Difficulties come when we limit ourselves to one communication model, the transfer of information. Often in missions we have emphasized, and rightly so, those who have "never heard." We desire to "go and tell" and call others to support and pray for our "telling." Though this emphasis is necessary, it may lead people to think that all we have to do is "take the gospel" to those who have never heard, make the message available. As mentioned earlier, in the transmission model of communication, the emphasis is on the message. My earliest books were about sharing the message, equipping literates to put the gospel message in a mode in which oral communicators can understand. Putting the message in an understandable mode, as important as it is, is only one step in helping someone accept Christ. True, one cannot accept if one has not heard. Hearing a message is not the same as accepting it or applying its truths to our lives, however. If hearing information equaled putting the information into practice, we would all be much more physically healthy!

Because of technology and the spread of Western education, much of the world is learning to practice the transmission style of communication. In collective societies, however, the transaction model of communication is preferred. Interestingly, even in individualistic societies where the transmission model of communication is practiced, employers are increasingly looking for those who are team players, those who are comfortable with the transaction model of communication.

In the transaction model of communication, the messenger and the receiver are active parts of the communication process. The major skill in the transaction communication model is listening rather than speaking. Listening not only occurs with the ears but also with the eyes. The messenger creates a relationship with the receiver, and it is through this relationship that the message passes. The messenger becomes attuned to the receiver and adjusts the message to the needs of the receiver. As we talk about missions, I know we have emphasized sharing and telling. Have we also emphasized listening?

It may be that we confuse "listening" with "agreeing." We know the truth and have little patience listening to untruths. Because we can think faster than someone can speak, instead of listening, we may use the time they are speaking to think of what we want to say next, especially if we are language learners. Listening respectfully does not mean agreeing, however.

Jesus was a wonderful listener. He knew how to ask questions so that others would share. His message came through in His caring attitude, not in just what He said. When He spoke to the Samaritan woman at the well, it was not long before she was telling Him her life history. Even though Jesus surely knew the subject of the men's conversation that He met on the road to Emmaus, Jesus asked them to share their thoughts. He listened. Jesus also knew when to keep silent. Even in the face of His accusers during his trial, He did not argue.

As a U.S. American and the product of my individualistic culture, I am comfortable being the one in control, speaking, sharing my message. I tend to look on silence as agreement. Silence is a space that is waiting to be filled. An ancient Chinese philosopher once said that those who speak do not know, implying that those who keep silent are really the knowledgeable ones. This belief has caused problems for Asian international students when they are faced with chattering U.S. American students in graduate seminars. Proverbs 17:27a says, "The intelligent person restrains his words…"

We need to learn to listen with our eyes as well as our ears. Listening with our eyes means being aware of body language. In the transaction model of communication, body language as well as silence are part of the communication and carry meaning.

Before we began our first storying group, my husband visited the chief of the village where we wanted to share Bible stories. Visiting just to "greet" is an important part of African culture. Marvin visited the chief about eight times, sitting with him, often in silence. Finally, the chief asked what Marvin wanted. Marvin said that we wanted permission to share the Bible stories in the village, and the chief readily agreed.

Listening denotes respect. I Peter 3:16 admonishes us to talk about the hope that is within us with gentleness and respect. We must listen to the stories of others with respect. Once, while storying to a group of women, an African man, the husband of two of the women in the group, decided to visit our gathering. That day, I shared the story of the Fall of Humanity. He nodded enthusiastically as I shared the story. He then pointed to the "Adam's apple" below his chin and said, "That is why we have this, because the fruit got stuck there." I nodded my head thoughtfully as each of the women looked at me. "That is interesting," I said. "Was that in the story?" I asked slowly.

He admitted it was not, but then added hopefully, "Maybe it will be in next week's story." I slowly shrugged my shoulders. I had not confirmed his story, but hopefully I had treated him with gentleness and respect.

What increases our respect for a person? Is it education, wealth, social position, age, job, fortitude? Do we still respect those who lack these qualities? If we do not respect those with whom we are sharing and we are unwilling to listen to the stories of their families or sit with them in silence, we have a problem that deserves our attention.

Telling a Story

There are professional Bible storytellers complete with an association, conference, and training program. Most of us will not become professional storytellers. We learn and tell stories not only because it benefits us personally but in order to share the story with others.

Though we are used to sharing personal stories as adults, many Christians associate Bible stories with their childhood. We may have fond memories of Vacation Bible School, Sunday School, or family devotions and remember the Bible stories shared there. If so, it is possible that our Bible storytelling schema includes an adult sharing a Bible story with a child. We must engage in critical thinking as we examine that schema. If we hunt for the assumptions, one assumption that could be part of our schema is that Bible stories are for children. Though we know this is not true, this assumption could be an unconscious part of our schema. Another assumption might be that stories are simple and not worthy of attention by Bible specialists. If we check those assumptions, we find them to be false. One African pastor testified how he had not been interested when he had heard of Bible storying because it seemed too simple. He could not see how sharing Bible stories would help people learn the doctrine necessary to understand salvation. After struggling to learn and tell a Bible story, however, his opinion changed dramatically.

In looking at these assumptions from the viewpoint of others, we consider our audience and their possible reactions to the manner in which we tell the story. In telling a Bible story, are we unconsciously casting our hearers into the role of children?

In a storying conference once, I decided to model how to tell a story to a group. I asked a few women to role-play my group. I sat on a chair as they sat on the floor surrounding me. It was not long after I began the story that I realized my phrasing and tone were one in which I would use with children. Interestingly, sitting on the floor around me, the women subtly changed their body language to mimic that of children. The unconscious adjustments in both my telling and their listening were influenced by our schemata. As soon as I realized what was happening, I stopped, explained to the group of women and the observers what was happening, and changed our seating arrangement. I circled chairs around me and asked the women to sit on the chairs. I instructed them to be conscious of their body language, that this was a group of adults. Beginning again, I became conscious of my tone and expression. It was a wonderful teaching moment.

Stories may be for children, but they are also for adults. Though we may not be conscious of it, as adults we speak in stories. We tell stories of our children or grandchildren, we tell stories of our car breaking down, stories of our do-it-yourself remodel, stories of a basketball team's comeback, and stories of surviving cancer. When we tell these stories, we do not alter our voice as an adult speaking to a child, and we do not adjust our body language. We do not treat our listeners as children, just because we are telling a story.

If we grew up surrounded by literate adults, it may be that the only nonliterates we knew were children. If so, we may unconsciously think of nonliterate adults in oral cultures as childlike. Global organizations often speak of "illiteracy" as a dreaded disease that must be wiped out. If that concept has influenced us, we may also think of nonliterate adults as deficient. If we unconsciously think of nonliterate adults in oral cultures as childlike and deficient, that belief will manifest itself in our voice and body language as we tell a Bible story. Even though nonliterate adults in oral cultures may be used to being treated like children or deficient by other literates, we must be conscious that we are treating nonliterates with the respect they deserve as adults. As a literate, I will always be an outsider in an oral culture. I accept that compared to them, I am "non-oral" just as they are "non-literate." If they accept to hear my story, then

I must tell it using the same tone and body language that I would use if telling the story to literate adults.

What do the following phrases have in common with each other, and how do they differ?

1. Once upon a time…

2. In a land far away…

3. You won't believe what happened to me last night…

4. Long, long, ago…

It is easy to see that examples #1, #2, and #4 are phrases we use as indicators that what is to follow is a fable or fairy tale, a story that is fictional. If a friend begins a conversation with phrase #3, we expect the rendition to be true. Each language has its own story markers as well. We must become familiar with those story markers and not use the ones that indicate a fictional story when we are sharing Bible stories.

Situational Stories

When we can verbalize our salvation story, are conscious of our faith stories, and have learned some Bible stories, the next step is to make ourselves available to be used. As God is at work in the world, I believe He schedules divine appointments. Our responsibility is to be available and ready to share. When we are equipped and available, opportunities abound. If we do not do the hard work necessary to become equipped, whether it be learning Bible stories or learning the language, we may miss the blessing of seeing God work through us.

The first step in situational sharing is becoming aware of situations in which we can share. Just as we talked about the importance of critical thinking in paying attention to assumptions, we must also become aware of the situations we encounter daily in the course of our lives where it would be natural for us to share. We may be used to going through our lives focused on our next appointment rather than stopping to see and seize opportunities. If we are equipped and available, I believe God will give us opportunities.

I once heard a speaker stress the importance of telling God when we are available and willing to be used. A blanket "use me Lord" once in the morning is necessary but does not ensure that we will remember that we said we are available. We may not be looking expectantly for God to work. This speaker told a story about being confined to home one day but deciding to tell God she was available if He wanted to use her. Her story included a call from an obscene phone caller, God's reminder that she said she was available and should not hang up, her witnessing to the surprised caller, and his ultimate salvation and service as a deacon at her church. It was a wonderful story, and it stuck with me (as stories tend to do).

One day when we lived in Wyoming where my husband and I were starting a church, I was home and for some reason, knew I could not leave the house. God brought the speaker's story to mind, and I decided to "give it a try." I prayed and told God that I was available, but since I could not leave the house, he would have to do something. I did not receive an obscene phone call, but several hours later there was a knock at the door. It was two elementary school girls, one of whom had attended our Vacation Bible School. She said, "This is my friend. We were just walking down the street and decided to stop to see you. Can you tell us how to become a Christian?" It is always amusing to me how we ask God to act, then when He does, we are surprised. I was definitely surprised as I invited them in to talk. What eventually ensued was a heartbreaking tale of the friend's sexual abuse at the hand of her stepfather. The friend had confided in the girl who had been to VBS. When they saw my house, they thought I might be able to help and began the conversation in a way they knew would catch my interest. That encounter began a saga filled with many tears. The abusive family and the girl disappeared in the night when they heard there was an investigation. It was very sad, and I have often thought of that girl, now a grown woman. When we had arrived to plant a church in the town, my husband had visited each house to introduce himself. The only family to slam the door in his face were a family of atheists. The wife in this family heard through the grapevine of my efforts to intervene on behalf of the abused girl and called me to say she appreciated "that I had the guts to stand up and do what I did." That phone call began a friendship that ultimately led to the salvation of all four people in that family as well as several in their extended family.

I do not want to give the impression that God always acts when we say we are available. Once, I had returned to the United States from Africa for a conference and a short vacation. I decided to fly to Salt Lake for a few days. As I stood in the airport in Dallas/Fort Worth, I looked around at the other passengers. Our plane was one with two seats on one side and three on the other. I had the aisle seat on the side with two seats. I was tired and grumpy as I looked around, very much in need of a vacation. There was a long list of passengers on the monitor waiting for a seat. Knowing the plane would be packed, I begrudgingly told God that I was available to witness if He wanted to put someone beside me. I boarded early and watched as people came down the aisle, wondering who God had chosen. As the plane took off, there was only one empty seat. It was beside me. I had to laugh as I realized there was no way that God was going to put someone beside me in the mood I was in. He wanted me to rest. I stretched out and slept. On the return trip, relaxed and in a much better mood, I eyed the others in the passenger lounge in the Salt Lake airport as we waited for our flight to be called. A few rows away, I spied what was obviously a group of young Mormon missionaries. I said, "Go ahead, Lord. Put one of them by me." He did. We had a good conversation. The young man was the leader of the group on their way to Brazil for two years. We talked about intercultural communication and living overseas. At one point in our conversation, I pointed out that his beliefs and mine were very different. He surprised me when he readily agreed. He said, "I used to go to Vacation Bible School with my neighbors, so I know what you believe." We enjoyed the rest of our conversation. I was content to know that God had put me in the young man's path, perhaps because the young man needed a friendly reminder of the gospel he had heard as a child and how his beliefs differed. I do not know what became of him or how God continued to work in his life. I do know that God wanted me to be one step in the young man's journey. When we are available, God may choose to use us, giving us amazing faith stories. He may also choose not to use us. Either way, it is God who is at work, but He can use sharpened tools much better than dull ones.

As described above, our first responsibility in situational sharing is to look for opportunities and be available in the normal routine of our lives. The second area where we can practice situational sharing is through intentional ministry, going out for the purpose of sharing. Intentional sharing also involves being available for God to use, but instead of sharing in the context of our daily lives, we go out looking for where God is at work and join Him there. Whether this is looking for a person of peace who can introduce us to others, looking for opportunities to pray, or looking for opportunities to share faith and Bible stories, intentional sharing must occur in an attitude of prayer. One friend described intentional ministry this way. "When I go into the market to buy something, I search for the thing, buy it, and leave. When I go into the market intent on ministry, I may buy something, but the whole time I'm looking around me, trying to see people as God would see them. I ask Him who I should approach, where I should sit, what I should say. I let Him orchestrate encounters, but I am always looking for opportunities."

When we share situationally in intentional ministry, there may be certain stories that are appropriate for particular situations. J. O. Terry, former global practitioner in Asia and a master of situational storying, has written a book on food stories that can be used during famine relief. He has also compiled story lists pertinent for use in other situations such as with women in grief. Being prepared with stories appropriate for specific situations, being aware, and seizing opportunities to share stories from God's Word is a necessary element of intentional sharing.

In this chapter, we have seen the importance of respectfully listening to the stories of others and establishing relationships. Sharing the gospel is not just about sharing the gospel message, it is also about sharing ourselves. We must keep in mind that when we tell Bible stories to adults that our speech and body language should not cast our listeners into the role of children. We must be equipped, knowing stories from God's Word that are pertinent to specific situations, conscious of how God is working in our lives giving us faith stories. We must become available, looking for situations in the context of our daily lives where we can share with others but also intentionally seeking the lost. God is still writing our story, full of conflict, full of God's provision. How many other characters he adds to our story is in large part, up to us – our preparedness, our availability, and our obedience.

Marie leaned forward, trying to count the women on the bench, their babies on their laps. She would have a long wait. She knew it was important for Anna to be weighed regularly, but she did not enjoy the hours of waiting at the clinic just to spend five minutes with the health worker. She grinned. She was beginning to sound like Stacey. She enjoyed Stacey's visits to her courtyard, the inquisitive Bryan on her back. Just yesterday, Stacey had told her that each day she prayed that God would use her, put someone in her path so that she could tell them of her faith. Marie had not tried that before. She was learning a lot from Stacey. Just then, the health worker appeared and called the first number. Marie glanced down at the block of wood she held in her hand, the number "45" burned into it. She sighed. Before she left the house to walk to the clinic, she had done as Stacey suggested and prayed that God would bring someone to her and show her what she needed to say. Even though she was a Christian, most of the women in the village were civil to her because she was married to Muhammad who was a relative of the chief. They did not mind if she was a Christian as long as he remained a Muslim. Just then, a veiled woman sat down beside her on the bench, her darting eyes the only thing visible to the world. The woman pulled an infant from her back and clutched him on her lap. His limbs were shrunken, his hair red from malnutrition. Marie took a deep breath. She had prayed and now this woman had sat down beside her. Anna squirmed in her arms. Marie knew God wanted her to say something, but how could she begin? Just then, the radio blared over the loudspeakers and she heard Muhammad's familiar voice giving announcements. "That's my husband," she said to the woman sitting next to her. The woman nodded. "There are some white people here who are trying to learn our language. My husband is teaching them and I am helping the woman practice. She has been reading me stories from God's Word. Would you like to hear a story about Jesus' power, how He healed a man who was weak and sick with leprosy?" The woman looked down at the sickly boy in her lap, then shrugged her shoulders. Marie began...

CHAPTER 9

Creation to Christ and Chronological Bible Storying

Stacie sat on the concrete floor beside the bloated body of Marie's aunt, Aminata. "Isn't there anything the doctors can do?" she asked Marie, who hovered behind her.

"They say at the clinic that they have tried everything. Perhaps they could treat her at the big hospital in the capital city, but it would be very difficult to transport her there. Marie leaned down and took her aunt's hand in her own. "Auntie," she said, "Are you awake? We came to visit you." The woman opened her eyes, and turned her head toward them, smiling slightly. "Thank you, Stacey, Marie. Where are your babies?" Marie smiled.

"With their fathers." Aminata shook her head.

"You know that isn't a man's job, to take care of children. Shame on both of you." Stacey tried to keep the smile from her face.

"We didn't want them to disturb you. Bryan does not stay still very long, and Anna is crawling everywhere." The older woman shrugged and let go of Marie's hand to straighten the wrinkled cloth that covered her.

"What is the purpose of your visit?" she asked, eyeing them. For several weeks, Stacey and Marie had been learning Bible stories, practicing them, then sharing them with Aminata. They had begun with stories in the Old Testament, but the afternoon before, Marie had confided in Stacey that she did not feel that Aminata had much time. They needed to present the gospel. Stacey and Mark had been working on a panoramic story of the Bible and Stacey had practiced it with Marie, but when Stacie had asked Marie to share the story with her aunt, Marie had refused.

"I have shared the gospel with her many times. I am her niece. I think she will take it more seriously if the story comes from you." At Stacey's glum expression, Marie had smiled. "Don't worry. I will be beside you, praying. I know you'll do fine."

"Auntie," Marie said. "We have been telling you stories from God's Word. You have seen how God created the world. Stacey has another story to share with you about God's plan. She needs to practice her language. Won't you listen?"

Of course," said the older woman. "What did you want to tell me little one?"

Continuing in our efforts to be equipped to share stories with the world, in this chapter we will first discuss how to tell a panoramic story from the Bible, a story which includes God's working from creation to the resurrection of Christ. This broad story, which can be used in situational sharing when one wishes to provide an overview of the gospel, is often called the Creation to Christ or Creation to Church story. Also in this chapter, we will look more at the evangelism method of Chronological Bible Storying (CBS) which was briefly introduced in the previous chapter. At the end of the chapter, we will consider how technology and the availability of audio recordings of Bible stories contribute to evangelism.

In the next chapter, we will briefly highlight an evangelism strategy called S-T4T which focuses on church planting. The panoramic Creation to Church story as well as a group of core stories are used in this program.

Creation to Christ Story

We have discussed how one can tell one's personal salvation story, faith stories, and biblical stories with few details or many details, depending on the situation and the needs of the hearers. In the same way, the panoramic story of God working through history can include as many or as few details as the storyteller wishes. A short version may take less than ten minutes. Once you have learned many stories from God's Word, you may wish to give more details in some parts.

Once while in Africa, I had to drive to a neighboring city for a conference and did not want to make the drive in the car by myself. It was not difficult to find friends of a friend to take advantage of a free ride. Among the group of people was a man whom I had never met, a Muslim. He appropriated the front seat beside me. I knew I had roughly two hours to story. My panoramic Creation to Christ story began in my hometown and ended as I stopped at our destination. During the trip, I had paused as we stopped the car to stretch our legs and grab snacks. He did not look bored, so I continued. The other people in the car, some of whom were fellow church members, listened also. When I left the Muslim man, he told me, "Now, I understand." I never saw him again so I do not know how God used His Word. I do know that we are promised that God's Word does not return to us empty.

I did not use the panoramic story much in my ministry but my husband, Marvin, used it quite frequently. The following is his version of the story as he told it to Africans struggling with issues of fear and power. I give it here as an example of what one can include in a panoramic story. This story is a witnessing tool and is a way of sharing the gospel message that includes God's working through history. As discussed earlier, when telling a Bible story we must be careful not to include any teaching that is not in the story. Because it is a witnessing tool and not intended to give the listeners Scripture they can carry in their minds, the Creation to Christ story may include explanations or teaching.

In the beginning God existed; there was no other living thing. He created heaven and earth using only His words. He created beings to serve Him in Heaven. We call these beings angels. God created the great objects that we see in the sky: the sun, the moon, and the stars. He created the dry ground that we call earth and all the plants that we know including plants and trees. Then He created the animals that roam upon it—both the wild and the domestic animals. He created the great waters and the many creatures that live in them. He created the birds that fly in the skies. Last of all God created the first man and the first woman. He placed them in a beautiful garden that He called Eden. There was a good relationship between them and God.

But not all relationships remained good. One of the angels that God had created rebelled against God and was cast out of heaven. He began to roam upon the earth. He was called Satan. Through a serpent, Satan tempted the first man and woman, and they decided to disobey God. As a result of their disobedience their eyes were opened, and they were afraid. They made clothes for themselves and hid from God in the garden. God knew what they had done, and He knew how to find them. He punished them for their disobedience and banished them from the garden. The result of their disobedience was that the good relationship between humankind and God was broken. The first man and woman were afraid of what would happen to them. God did not, however, forget the people He created. He continued to love them.

Much time passed and the man and woman had children who also had children. They became numerous upon the earth. These children also were fearful. They were afraid of the many demons upon the earth. They feared they might anger the spirits of their ancestors. They feared most of all that God would forget them. Because of these fears, God permitted the people to offer animal sacrifices to Him in an effort to re-establish the good relationship. Ultimately, the power of these blood sacrifices was not enough to make the relationship with God right. It would take an even greater sacrifice.

God continued to remember the people He had created. He continued to love them. One day, God approached a man named Abraham and made some promises to him. First of all, God told Abraham to leave his home, his family, and the idol worshipers where he lived and to go to a land that God would show to Abraham. God promised to give Abraham many descendants and make of him a great nation. God promised to give Abraham a great name, and He promised that through Abraham, all the people on earth would be blessed. Abraham and God had a good relationship because Abraham put his trust in God and not in sacrifices alone.

When Abraham and his wife, Sarah, had lived a long time together God finally gave them a son. They were very happy but one day God told Abraham to go to a mountain and to sacrifice his son there on an altar. This made Abraham very fearful for he loved his son and did not want to lose him. Abraham obeyed God and with his knife in hand at the moment of slaying his son, God stopped him. God demonstrated His own love and power by providing a ram as a sacrifice to substitute for Abraham's son.

Abraham's son had children and those children had other children until they became a great people on the earth just as God had promised. They were known as the people of God but they continued to disobey God. They worshipped idols and were afraid of the demons and spirits. They were not faithful to God who had created them.

God sent spokesmen called prophets to His people to teach them the correct way to worship God their creator. The prophets tried to persuade the people not to offer sacrifices to others gods and spirits. The prophets told them that they should remain faithful to God and that one day God would send them a Savior. The people were to put their trust in the Savior for He would suffer the consequences of their sins.

The prophets also foretold that this Savior would be accepted by some and rejected by others. They foretold that finally He would die for the people in their place, as a sacrifice for their sins. But that was not the end of the story because He would conquer death, rise from the grave, and live again. The people were encouraged when they learned that they no longer had to be afraid because the power of this Savior was greater than Satan or any of his demons. His power was greater than any of the spirits of the ancestors who might try to do them harm.

The people waited many years for this Savior to come. Finally, He did arrive as promised. He was born to a young woman who had never been with a man. God made this happen by the power of his Holy Spirit. He was called Jesus (Issa, Yesu, etc.) When He was grown, He began to teach the people about God who had sent Him. He demonstrated His power by healing the sick by placing His hand on them, by commanding demons to come out of people, by giving sight to the blind, and even by raising the dead.

This Savior called on the people to believe on Him and to put their trust in Him. He told them that there were many dwelling places in His father's house and that He would take those who trusted Him to live with Him there. Many did trust. Many did not. Some hated Him and finally rose up and arrested Him and beat Him and mistreated Him and spit on Him. They killed Him just as the prophets had said. But, Jesus came back to life on the third day just as God had promised by the prophets He had sent to the people.

After Jesus came back to life, He spent the next 40 days teaching His followers what they must do. He told them that He must leave them but that He would send the Holy Spirit as a Comforter to be with them. On the last day, Jesus was taken up to heaven and the people saw Him no more. As His followers were looking up to heaven, two angels appeared and told them that Jesus would return one day in the sky.

I follow Jesus. If you would like to become Jesus' follower, I can tell you more about Jesus and how you can become His follower. Then you, too, can put an end to fear and begin to experience the power of Jesus.

Chronological Bible Storying (CBS)

My husband and I were some of the first Southern Baptist missionaries to use CBS as a ministry tool in West Africa in the late 1980s. Our then field leader, Bill Bullington, asked us to try CBS, an evangelization program designed for use with those who could not read the Bible for themselves. At a CBS conference the following year, Jim Slack and J.O. Terry introduced CBS to other personnel in West Africa. At the conference, they taught the theory, and my husband and I provided examples from our efforts. Our experiences with the method and the way in which God worked to bring people to Himself, in spite of our ineptitude, have been chronicled elsewhere. This experience with CBS was my first exposure to orality and the world of nonliterates. Although I had majored in Speech in college and taken numerous communication courses, the concept that there was another world in which people learned and communicated without literacy was new to me. The realization that I was ignorant of their reality began a journey of learning more about this world and those who inhabited it. In 1996, I wrote a manual about CBS which I used to train West African church leaders and missionary personnel to use the method. The following is taken largely from that manual.

As discussed briefly in Chapter Eight, Chronological Bible Storying, also called CBS or storying, is a method of communicating biblical truths by presenting Bible stories in the order that they happened in time. After telling the story and depending upon the purpose of the storying set (evangelism, discipleship, or church planting) the storyteller, a storyer, asks questions to guide the listeners to discover truths in the stories. Different from situational storying, CBS is a comprehensive witnessing program designed to meet the needs of oral communicators. CBS reaches not only those who cannot read or write but also those who prefer to communicate through listening and speaking rather than reading or writing.

There are several criteria for choosing which stories should make up a storying set. First, stories are chosen because they tell about a major biblical event and help the listeners build a chronological framework upon which they can "hang" future stories. For example, including a story about David gives the listeners a reference point that can be used later to return and "fill in" multiple stories about David. Second, stories are chosen because they address particular bridges or barriers in the listeners' worldview. Understanding the listeners' current beliefs, some of which may be close to biblical truth, allows us to choose stories that bridge those beliefs. For example, the Creation story bridges the Islamic belief that the world was created by God while at the same time expressing the true, biblical nature of God. This story serves as a bridge between the Bible and their beliefs. It is also important to choose biblical stories that confront those beliefs that do not agree with the Bible, beliefs that serve as barriers to accepting the gospel message. For listeners who believe that Jesus was only a prophet and not God, it is important to tell stories of Jesus forgiving sins and doing miracles, acts that only God could do, in order to confront that barrier. The third criteria for choosing stories is selecting those which contain truths that correspond with the purpose of the storying set.

Evangelism Track

The truths brought out through the Evangelism Track are those truths which will show people that they are sinful, condemned, and helpless before God. The truths of the nature of God and the salvation provided in Jesus also help people come to faith in Christ. Because unbelievers are often knowledgeable about witchcraft and demons, truths about Satan help them learn about this enemy.

One of the beauties of storying is that listeners hear the stories of the Old Testament and learn of God's love which He showed over and over to the rebellious Hebrew people. Listeners come to the realization that just like the Hebrews, they have rebelled against God and are lost, sinners condemned before God. It is at that point that they hear of the hope in Christ through the stories of the New Testament. As stories are shared in chronological order, listeners often fall in love with Jesus, are heartbroken at His arrest and crucifixion, and have renewed hope and understanding with the story of Jesus' Resurrection and the Coming of the Holy Spirit at Pentecost. With this final story, having been convicted that they are lost, understanding that Jesus is God and their only hope, many accept to become followers of Christ.

Evangelism Track Truths

The following are the truths that are brought out through the stories in the Evangelism Track.

GOD

1. There is only one God.
He is Spirit. He reveals Himself to us as God the Father, God the Son, and God the Holy Spirit.

2. God is the creator of everything.
He is active, living, and present. He is interested in all that we are and do.

3. God communicates with people.
God inspired men through the Holy Spirit to write down His Word, the Bible. God communicates with us through His Word. The Holy Spirit helps us to understand the Bible, to recognize truth, and to realize that we are sinners.

4. God is everywhere.
God is not far away. We cannot hide from God.

5. God is all-powerful.
God can do anything. He overcomes all who are against Him. He is always victorious.

6. God knows everything.
God knows our desires, our needs, and our thoughts.

7. God is holy and righteous.

God Himself is the standard for goodness. Because God is righteous, He will never lower His standard of holiness nor accept anything other than the full payment for our sin.

8. God is loving, merciful, and gracious.

God showed His love by providing the perfect sacrifice for our sins. God is quick to forgive and wants all people to know Him.

9. God hates sin.

Because God is holy, He cannot allow sin to go unpunished. He will judge us for everything we do and say.

10. God fulfills his promises.

God is truth. If God says He will do something, He will do it.

HUMANKIND

1. Humankind was created in the image of God.

Because of this, we are different from the animals. Each man and woman has a soul and can know God.

2. Humankind are sinners.

Humankind chose to disobey God and thus to sin. We need God and are helpless to save ourselves.

3. Humankind can come to God only according to God's will and plan.

God gave humankind the Law so that we could understand what sin is. God requires a sacrifice and the shedding of blood to cover sin. The only sacrifice and shedding of blood that God will accept is the perfect sacrifice of Jesus.

SIN

1. Sin is failure to do what God wants, whether by rebellion or ignorance.

Sin is following our will or other people's will instead of God's will.

2. Sin causes separation and death.

The punishment for sin is death.

SATAN

1. Satan fights against God and God's will.

Satan rebelled against God and knows that one day God will punish Satan forever.

2. Satan is a liar and a deceiver.

Satan is the father of lies. He puts lies in people's hearts to keep them from God.

3. Satan hates humankind.

Satan is the ruler of this world. He wants all people to follow him so that they will not obey God.

JESUS

1. Jesus Christ is God.

Jesus Christ and God the Father are one. Jesus, the eternal Son of God, came to earth in the form of a man to reveal God to us.

2. Jesus Christ is man.

Jesus was born of the Holy Spirit and the virgin Mary so that He could live as a man on earth.

3. Jesus Christ is holy and righteous.

Even as a man, Jesus was without sin.

4. Jesus Christ is the promised Savior.

Jesus' birth, life, death, and resurrection were foretold in the Old Testament.

5. Jesus Christ is the only Savior.

Because Jesus is God and because He lived a sinless life on earth, He is the only acceptable sacrifice for our sins. We can have forgiveness of sin, become God's children, and receive eternal life by believing in Jesus, repenting of our sins, accepting the death of Jesus as our sacrifice, and following Jesus.

How many stories are in a typical Evangelism Track? I found that in my situation, I needed about 52 stories to address the people's worldview barriers in an African animistic context. In a situation where the people were Muslim, I added three more stories about obedience, bringing the story total to 55. Other storyers believe they can be effective with fewer stories. Others add more stories. The following are the stories I told in my Evangelism Track.

Evangelism Track for an African Traditional Religion Context:

1. **God's Word, the Bible**. 2 Timothy 3:16; 2 Peter 1:20-21
2. **The Spirit World and Satan**. Nehemiah 9:6; Job 38:4-7; Psalm 99:1-3; Psalm 103:19-21; Isaiah 45:12; Nahum 1:2-3; Luke 10:18; John 8:44; 12:31; Ephesians 2:2; 6:11-12; Colossians 1:15-16; 1 Timothy 3:6; 1 Peter 5:8; 1 John 3:8; Jude 6; Revelation 12:7-9; 20:10
3. **The Creation**. Genesis 1:1-2:3
4. **Adam and Eve**. Genesis 1:27-2:25, 3:20

35. **Prophecies of Isaiah and Micah.** Isaiah 6:1-8; 7:13-14; 8:19-22; 9:1-7; 11:1-3, 10; 40:1-5; 42:1-9; 52:13-15; 53; Micah 1:1; 5:1-5a
36. **John's Birth; The Announcement of Jesus' Birth.** Luke 1:5-45, 57-79
37. **The Birth of Jesus.** Matthew 1:18-25; Luke 2:1-20
38. **Jesus in the Temple.** Luke 2:21-52
39. **The Baptism of Jesus.** Luke 3:1-18; Matthew 3:13-17
40. **The Temptation of Jesus.** Matthew 4:1-11; Luke 4:14-30
41. **Jesus and his Disciples.** Luke 5:1-16; 6:12-16
42. **The Parable of the Sower.** Mark 4:1-20
43. **Jesus Heals a Demon-possessed Man.** Mark 5:1-20
44. **Jesus Calms the Storm and Feeds the Five Thousand.** Luke 8:22-25; John 6:1-15
45. **Jesus and Nicodemus.** John 3
46. **Jesus Heals a Blind Man.** John 9
47. **Jesus Raises Lazarus from the Dead.** John 11
48. **Jesus Announces his Death.** Luke 18:31-34; John 14; 15
49. **The Last Supper and Jesus' Arrest.** Luke 21:5-38; 22:1-53
50. **The Crucifixion.** Luke 22:54-71; Matthew 27:1-10, 27-31; Luke 23
51. **The Resurrection.** Luke 24:1-49; Acts 1:3-11
52. **The Holy Spirit Comes at Pentecost.** Acts 1:15-26; 2
53. **Invitation to Accept Christ.** Romans 1:16-25; 2:5-6; 3:20-26; 6:6-12; 6:23; 10:1-13

Evangelism Track for an African Islamic context

1. **The Creation.** Genesis 1:1 - 2:3
2. **Adam and Eve.** Genesis 1:27-2:25, 3:20
3. **The Spirit World and Satan.** Nehemiah 9:6; Job 38:4-7; Psalm 99:1-3; Psalm 103:19-21; Isaiah 45:12; Nahum 1:2-3; Luke 10:18; John 8:44; 12:31; Ephesians 2:2; 6:11-12; Colossians 1:15-16; 1 Timothy 3:6; 1 Peter 5:8; 1 John 3:8; Jude 6; Revelation 12:7-9; 20:10
4. **The Fall of Humankind.** Genesis 3
5. **Cain and Abel.** Genesis 4
6. **The Flood.** Genesis 6-9:17
7. **The Tower of Babel.** Genesis 9:1, 18-19; 11:1-9

37. **Jesus in the Temple.** Luke 2:21-52
38. **The Baptism of Jesus.** Luke 3:1-18; Matthew 3:13-17
39. **The Temptation of Jesus.** Matthew 4:1-11; Luke 4:14-30
40. **Jesus and his Disciples.** Luke 5:1-16; 6:12-16
41. **The Parable of the Sower.** Mark 4:1-20
42. **Jesus Heals a Demon-possessed Man.** Mark 5:1-20
43. **Jesus Calms the Storm and Feeds the Five Thousand.** Luke 8:22-25; John 6:1-15
44. **Jesus and Nicodemus.** John 3
45. **John the Baptist Questions Jesus.** Luke 3:19-20; Matthew 11:2-13, 25-30; Mark 6:17-29; Mark 6:14-16
46. **Jesus, the Bread of Life.** John 6:14-40, 47-54, 60-71
47. **Jesus and the Religious Leaders.** Matthew 12:1-14; Mark 3:20-26, 31-35; Matthew 12:15-21
48. **What Makes Someone Unclean?** Mark 7:1-8, 14-23; Luke 11:37-46; 12:1-9, 49-53
49. **Jesus Heals a Blind Man.** John 9
50. **Jesus Raises Lazarus from the Dead.** John 11
51. **Jesus Announces his Death.** Luke 18:31-34; John 14; 15
52. **The Last Supper and Jesus' Arrest.** Luke 21:5-38; 22:1-53
53. **The Crucifixion.** Luke 22:54-71; Matthew 27:1-10, 27-31; Luke 23
54. **The Resurrection.** Luke 24:1-49; Acts 1:3-11
55. **The Holy Spirit Comes at Pentecost.** Acts 1:15-26; 2
56. **Invitation to Accept Christ.** Romans 1:16-25; 2:5-6; 3:20-26; 6:6-12; 6:23; 10:1-13

Multiple resources now abound for use in preparing story lists. Paul Koehler designed a set of stories for use in India based on the major biblical characters, bringing out the truths needed for salvation as reflected through the stories of God's encounter with these characters. He discusses his experience in his book, *Telling God's Story with Power*.

Discipleship Track

The Discipleship Track builds on the truths revealed through the Evangelism Track and adds new truths that help the listeners understand what it means to be a follower of Jesus. The Discipleship Track manual I wrote for West African leaders takes truths from the Gospel of John, truths Jesus wants His disciples to know and things Jesus wants His disciples to do.

Discipleship Track Truths (from John)

Jesus wants His disciples to KNOW that:

1. Jesus loves them.

2. They are God's children and belong to Him.

3. They are saved from sin and free in Christ.

4. Jesus has conquered Satan.

5. They have passed from death to eternal life with Jesus.

6. The Holy Spirit is in them, teaching them and giving them power over Satan.

7. They no longer walk in darkness but walk in the light.

8. They will be persecuted because they have decided to follow Jesus.

9. Their failures are forgiven when they repent.

10. Jesus calls some to lead other disciples. These leaders are to serve others and help them to be true disciples.

Things Jesus wants His disciples to DO:

1. Trust in Jesus.

2. Pray.

3. Love Jesus.

4. Obey Jesus' commands.

5. Be free from the slavery of sin.

6. Follow Jesus and remain in Him every day.

7. Have peace and not be afraid.

8. Have a full and joyful life.

9. Love one another.

10. Serve others.

11. Confess their faith and testify to others.

12. Bear much fruit (Bring other people to Jesus).

13. Be in unity with other believers.

Other Storying Tracks

To understand the concept of storying tracks, it helps to visualize a brick wall. We cannot see the foundational layer of bricks, but without a true and straight foundation, the wall will be crooked or topple. That foundational layer is the Evangelism Track. Understanding the gospel message and with a chronology of the Bible from the Old Testament to the Coming of the Holy Spirit at Pentecost, believers have a strong biblical foundation they can carry in their minds. Covering the Evangelism Track but also foundational, is the Discipleship Track. In this group of stories, the truths of the Evangelism Track are reinforced and believers learn new truths about what it means to live as a disciple of Jesus.

In the Church Planting Track, normally a set of stories from the book of Acts, listeners discover God's plan for the early church. The people are encouraged to meet together and come to church just as new believers were gathered into church in Acts. Once the foundation has been set, future rows of bricks – stories – can cover any topic in the life of the church or the believer. A group of stories on tithing can be compiled, as can one on marriage or childrearing. For use with leaders in West Africa, I suggested a series of stories from events in the life of David that brought out truths about leadership – both what a leader should and should not do. Just as one would not begin building a brick wall by starting a line of bricks in the air without a proper foundation, so the stories in the Evangelism Track – leading to conviction and salvation – are necessary before stories which talk about how to live as a believer.

Storying Sessions

Chronological Bible Storying was designed to be used with a relatively stable population of oral communicators who are either resistant to the gospel or say they are Christians but are steeped in syncretism. As first envisioned, the storyer would invest in the people, learn the language, and build relationships. After discovering the people's worldview and belief system, the storyer would build a set of stories that confronted the people's worldview and helped them understand the truths of the gospel. The stories would be revealed, one by one, through story sessions.

There are generally four parts to the typical storying session:

1. Introduction:

The session is treated like an event. The storyer catches up on the news and happenings since the previous session then leads the conversation into a review of stories that have been told earlier. The storyer may give the people a listening task, something to listen for in the story such as how God fulfilled His promise to Abraham. The storyer tells a transition story, tying the current story to the one before and explaining any difficult concepts that the people might encounter and need to understand in order to understand the current story (like "Scribe").

2. Signal that the Story is from the Bible:

In traditional CBS, the storyer signals that the Bible story is beginning by taking a Bible in hand. This action demonstrates that the story is from God's Word and not from the speaker himself or herself. The storyer quotes or reads a few verses from the Bible story. In situations where the storyer is not literate or the Bible has not been translated into the language, the storyer needs to help the listeners understand that the story is from God's written Word, the Bible.

3. Tell the Story:

Advice on telling a story has already been discussed in Chapter Eight. In the traditional story session, the storyer holds the Bible as he or she tells the story in his or her own words. Holding the Bible while telling the story distinguishes the Bible story from the discovery time following the story.

4. Lead the Discovery Time:

If a listening task was given to the listeners before the scripture reading, the storyer begins the discovery time by asking about the task. The listeners are led to retell the story, one helping another with the storyer correcting any errors. The storyer then asks factual questions which can be answered from story events. For example, listeners can answer the question "What are some of the things that God created?" because the answers were given in the Creation Story. Discovery questions follow factual questions. After the listeners have listed some of the items God created, asking a discovery question such as, "What does this tell us about God?" requires that the listeners draw conclusions. The storying session should end before the group grows restless and quits listening. Giving a hint about the next story increases interest for the next session.

Discovery questions may be a new type of question for some listeners, but listeners can be taught the skill of drawing conclusions. In the above example, if the listeners named several items that God created but balked at drawing conclusions about God, I would ask, "Does the fact that God created the sun show us that God is weak?" They would easily respond in the negative. I would then say, "Then what does it show us?" Usually, they could respond, "God is all powerful." Once when going through this series of questions with my neighbor after telling her the Creation Story, I asked several factual questions such as "What did God create?" and "What did God see about these things after He created them?" She easily named several items and responded that God saw that they were good. When I asked what that told us about God, she answered quickly, "You know I am just a woman. I cannot know God." I assured her that God gave us these stories so that we could know Him. I then asked if the things God made were bad. She said that they were not. I asked, "What does the fact that God made good things for us tell us about God?" She answered, "He loves us." Surprise lit her face as she realized that even as a woman, she could know something about God. Surprise turned to joy as she realized the thing that she had discovered about God was that He loved her. I had not told her God loved her. She had discovered that fact herself from the story, something she had never known before. The concept of God's love was not a belief in the religion she followed.

Knowing how to build discovery questions on factual questions is a skill, and helping people respond who are not used to discovering truths for themselves can be challenging. It is wonderful when they "get it" however, and their faces reflect the wonderment of personal discovery. I have personally witnessed what I term "a crack in their worldview" when people respond aloud to a question and then realize that their response goes against their current beliefs. Leading a discovery time in this way is just that, leading. The storyer has a particular purpose with particular truths in mind that he or she wants the listeners to discover. Because this type of discovery time involves analysis and drawing conclusions, it may be more comfortable for literates.

Many storyers feel uncomfortable using factual and discovery questions during the discovery time because it is difficult for nonliterates and some storyers consider it too directive. Many prefer to ask a limited number of general questions that leave the discussion open. For example, they may ask what the listeners liked about the story as well as what was difficult to understand in the story. They may ask what characteristics of God the listener saw in the story or what truths the listeners saw that they can apply to their lives. Some storyers do not ask any particular questions but lead the listeners in a general discussion of the story.

Going through the stories of the Evangelism Track as I practiced CBS can be a long process because the stories confront the listeners' existing schemata, their current beliefs as to the nature of God and salvation, and present the gospel fully, slowly changing the listeners' schemata. As envisioned, going through an Evangelism Tack of stories that fulfill these criteria can take from three to twelve months. That seems like a long time, especially to U.S. Americans. But it is not a long time if we realize we are tearing down Satan's lies and giving the people an opportunity to put God's truth in their hearts. The storyer does not normally skip ahead to discuss the end of the story before the people know the beginning of the story. That means not introducing Jesus until He is revealed in the New Testament, though the truths about Him leading up to His coming are brought out in the stories. The last story in the Old Testament is usually a story highlighting the prophecies of Jesus' birth.

In a situation where the people have never heard the gospel, it is very difficult for a Christian not to mention Jesus at the beginning of storying. The Christian already knows the end of the story and wants to tell others the end of the story, too. In traditional CBS, the storyer teaches as God revealed His plan in history. God did not tell the Israelites all that would happen to them. He wanted the Israelites to see that they needed to obey Him. It took time for them to learn that they were lost and that they could be saved only by accepting Jesus as their sacrifice. For those who have never heard the gospel in a way they can understand, it will take time for them to learn that they, too, are lost. When they understand truths about God, humankind, Satan, sin, and Jesus, truths that may go against what they currently believe, and when they know that they are lost and only Jesus can save them, they will really understand the gospel.

Sometimes people are drawn to the religion of Christianity because they want something from God. They want answers to their prayers. They want more money, a better job, or healing. It is possible they never really understand that they are lost. They are still the god of their lives, and they may look on Christianity as a way of fulfilling their needs. Unless they learn differently, if, after they are baptized, they do not get more money, a better job, or healing, they may reject Christianity. People like this were probably never saved. They did not understand that it does not matter if they never get more money, a better job, or healing. It only matters that they are lost and Jesus is the only way to salvation.

The concept that "it is not all about us" is a difficult concept for everyone. On a flight in the United States not long ago, I sat beside a man from Orange County in California. He shared stories of some of his rich and eccentric neighbors and his attempt to be "normal" while surrounded by the wealthy. By his stories, I knew that he was not a Christian. I asked about his church background, and he said that he and his wife occasionally attended a large non-denominational church where his son was enrolled in preschool. Ours was a short flight, and I did my best to present the gospel. On the back of the headrest of the seat in front of me, I traced two circles with my finger. I told him that for most people, we see ourselves as the center of the circle and God is in a smaller circle outside ours, rotating around us, there to help us when we need it. He nodded in agreement. I then said that actually, it is not about us but about God. I crossed out the circle with us in the center and traced a "G" in the center of the second circle. I told the man that God is the one in the center of the circle and we are in a small circle on the outside. We must have a bridge, which is Jesus, to become acceptable to God. It is not about us. It is about God. The man looked at me quizzically, then bluntly and emphatically exclaimed, "Well, good luck with that!" I laughed, and agreed with him that this was not the message that the world wanted to hear. He shook his head because what I had explained was far from his humanistic beliefs. I could tell that he was also challenged by my words, however.

Understanding Truths

Helping people learn how to analyze a story and draw out truths is a learned skill. Whereas those with a U.S. American education may learn this skill in preschool, other education systems may not teach this skill until later grades. Nonliterates may never have been taught this skill, and it may be uncomfortable for them. Stories and proverbs rather than analysis and opinion are often preferred in collectivistic cultures because they are nonconfrontational. Rather than express feelings directly, by telling a story, the listener must interpret the story and draw his or her own conclusions. If I were to ask a nonliterate woman's opinion of her neighbor, she probably would not say that her neighbor was kind and gracious or mean-tempered. Instead, the woman would tell me a story demonstrating the neighbor's behavior. If she told me a story of the neighbor being mean-tempered, I would be left to make up my own mind as to the neighbor's character. It does not mean the nonliterate woman has not analyzed her neighbor's behavior or does not have an opinion. It does mean that the woman is not willing to share her opinion of her neighbor publicly.

We can teach the skill of drawing out truths from Scripture. As illustrated by helping my friend learn that God loves us, we can ask a series of "yes" and "no" questions. We can also "think aloud," modeling the mental steps we go through to arrive at conclusions. The skill of analysis is helpful when interpreting Scripture. My friend was amazed when she discovered that God loved her. As literates schooled in the U.S. American school system, however, we also need to learn the skill of sharing stories instead of analysis. Before I knew much about oral cultures, I did not mind sharing my opinion with anyone who would listen. I quickly drew conclusions and had no problem stating those conclusions. As I learned more about other cultures, I realized that there are rarely simple answers to complex problems. As I have seen the beauty of collectivistic cultures, more and more I share my opinion through stories. Sometimes because U.S. Americans tend to want an analysis and "the bottom line," I may give my opinion then tell a story to support it.

Technology and CBS

Modern technology has allowed tremendous advances in the area of Chronological Bible Storying. Now, many story sets are available digitally through audio recordings as well as video recordings. Some story sets are available on SIM cards or memory chips that people can listen to on their phones. It is not necessary to spend as much time repeating the story in a storying session if people have access to a recording of the story. People who are not open to hearing our salvation story or faith story may be willing to listen privately to Bible stories.

Before we left the mission field, we hired an African evangelist who worked at a Christian hospital to record all 52 stories in the local language onto cassettes. The recordings included the stories and a series of questions and answers following each story. The evangelist's first exposure to storying was when we asked him to record the stories. He came from a family of Muslim leaders and had been rejected because of his faith. Prior to agreeing to record the stories, he learned that he had a terminal illness. He told us that though he had been an evangelist for years and read the Bible through on multiple occasions, he had never really understood the depths of God's love until he recorded the stories and saw how God continually reached out to a rebellious nation. Though the doctors were amazed, God allowed this man to live long enough to record all of the stories, a six-month process. He had been determined to finish. He told us that he felt that the recordings were his legacy, a way to reach his people after his death. At his funeral, his family, many of the Muslim leaders, came to town. Though it was a Christian funeral, the procession went by the house of his Muslim relatives to greet them. I was amongst the crowd which was addressed by one of the older men. He said that he finally understood the evangelist, that there was no problem with him, that he had always been a good son. Then, he gave an African blessing that translates roughly, "May his work continue." I was shocked. The next day, I asked someone at the hospital if I had heard correctly. I was told that the night before the funeral, someone had given the family members a set of the Bible stories on cassette tape. The stories totaled about ten hours. Several members of the family stayed up all night listening to the stories told by a familiar voice they had not heard for many years. In death, through the recording of the stories, the evangelist was able to accomplish what he could not during his life. His family finally understood his faith. They did not embrace it, but they understood.

Even though recorded stories are available, there should still be an emphasis on learning the stories, especially for those who do not have access to a printed Bible. Technology fails. Batteries die. Cassettes warp. SIM cards become damaged. Hiding God's Word in our cell phones is not the same thing as hiding it in our hearts. Rather than a repository of information, recorded stories should be memory aids as we learn the stories. Friends shared that some local leaders had become convinced that the storyer who was recorded could tell the story much better than they. Instead of telling the story, the storyers began taking cassette players and playing a storying cassette for the group. It was not long before people stopped attending. Sitting in a circle listening to a recorded voice was not the same as someone sitting with them and engaging them by telling a Bible story.

CBS in an Urban Setting

CBS in an urban setting can be challenging. While gathering a group to tell and listen to Bible stories is ideal, it is not easy to gather a group outdoors in the city because of curious passers-by, traffic, and the general bustle of urban living. Meeting in a courtyard may be difficult because landlords are often from the dominant religion and forbid people gathering if they know the Bible is involved. Meeting inside a house has its own perils because of suspicions raised when people of different sexes are seen entering a building together. Public buildings may not be affordable. Unbelievers hesitate to be seen at places of Christian worship. Field personnel may offer their homes in the beginning, but problems ensue when group members accept Christ and a church needs to be formed. Even when an appropriate place is found, people work at odd hours. Distractions abound. With a special moving of the Spirit, these challenges can, of course, be overcome.

Rather than attempting to gather a traditional CBS group, an appropriate use of recorded stories can prove helpful. If recorded stories are not available in the languages spoken, then seeing that they become available is an important priority. An urban environment is conducive to group listening. Sound penetrates. Recorded stories in the hands of church members who play them at home becomes an opportunity to witness to neighbors. Giving cassettes or memory cards of stories a few at a time allows the giver an excuse for a return visit for a discussion of the stories and the gift of the next stories. If urban personnel have a collection of stories in different languages, they may find that older people who have left their village to live with a relative in the city are hungry for the sound of their language. Listening to the stories in their own language can be a powerful witness.

In an urban setting, including storying in a group that meets for another purpose can be effective. I have used storying with a group of literate young men in high school who were excited about demonstrating their reading prowess. I kept a stack of French Bibles handy. When the group met, I passed out the Bibles, and they read the story passage. Then I told the story in my own words. We not only discussed the questions from the storying lesson, we also discussed a relevant topic of interest. For example, after the story of Creation we talked about evolution as it was presented in school. After the story of the Creation of Adam and Eve we discussed elements of marriage. Those in school who are faced with passing an English exam may appreciate the opportunity of hearing the stories and answering the questions in English. Nonliterate women who sit all day in market stalls may enjoy listening to a roaming storyer who passes from stall to stall sharing a story.

Because church members in urban settings have multiple networks, it can be effective to equip church members to use CBS, letting them take the lead in forming story listening groups. Training church members in CBS is not only an outreach tool, it is an effective discipleship tool for the church.

Building on the relationship ties from the village to an urban area is a strategy that is often neglected. When a believer from a village moves to the city, there should be follow-up. Often there are city neighborhoods that consist of people from one village with much travel back and forth from the village to the city. If people in the village have been involved in a storying group, they may want to continue that in the city and may provide access for a storyer to go to their neighborhood.

Personnel who speak a particular local language may also find a special welcome in the urban neighborhoods that use that language. My ability to speak a local language meant I was often ushered into inner sanctums, hidden places in the city that can go unnoticed, simply because the inhabitants were entertained by this foreigner who spoke their language. As my ministry was mainly in rural areas, I was limited by the amount of time I could spend with the city dwellers. Strategy that allows personnel from a given rural area to be invited to use CBS in an urban area with those who share his or her language can prove fruitful.

CBS in an urban setting presents unique challenges. Instead of asking that a group meet at the convenience of the storyer, often the storyer must become the mover, going from small group to small group, sharing stories whenever possible. With prayer, the leading of the Spirit, and a willingness to be flexible, the challenges of using CBS in an urban context can be met.

***

"What happened in the story between Jacob, Esau, and their father?" Mark asked. Muhammad sat comfortably in the chair beside the couch, Bryan playing with some trucks at his feet. Muhammad reeled off a suitable answer from the story he had just heard, thinking of the money he was making helping Mark learn the language. For weeks, Mark had been telling him Bible stories, practicing before Mark told the stories to the men in the late afternoon where they gathered in front of the store downtown to play cards. Muhammad didn't mind hearing them twice. A twinge went through him. Mark was able to communicate well, now. What if Mark decided he didn't need him anymore? He had come to depend on the salary.

"What happened in the dream that Jacob had?" Mark asked. It was easy to describe the angels and God's promise to Jacob to be with him and his descendants.

"How do we become acceptable to God?" Mark asked. Muhammad didn't hesitate but gave the answer he had believed for years. "By our good actions."

"Name Jacob's good actions that made him acceptable to God." Muhammad opened his mouth to answer, then closed it slowly as he thought about the story and the previous stories of Jacob. Jacob had lied to his father and tricked his brother. He had to run from his home in fear. None of his actions were good. Why had God come to him? Muhammad looked up to see Mark watching him carefully.

"Jacob didn't do anything good."

"Then why did God come to him and make promises to him?" Mark asked seriously as he leaned closer, waiting for Muhammad's answer. Muhammad hesitated, shaking his head slightly.

"I suppose it was because God wanted to. It was part of His plan," he said slowly. Suddenly, Muhammad stood up. "I just remembered I am supposed to go by the radio station," he said abruptly. He felt like his body was on fire. He hurried out the door and down the path, not wanting Mark to see how much the story had disturbed him.

CHAPTER 10

Evangelism, Discipleship, and Church

"**W**hat have you done to my husband?" Marie asked Stacey after they had exchanged greetings.

"What do you mean?"

"He has never been very religious, but suddenly he is praying five times a day, and he has gone to Friday prayers at the mosque for several weeks now. I thought that being around you would make him want to go less, not more," Marie said forcefully. Stacey took Bryan from her back and watched him carefully as he ran toward Anna who was sitting on a woven plastic mat in the shade.

"I don't know...unless..."

"What?"

"Mark said a few weeks ago that Muhammad was really touched by the story of Jacob's Dream, especially when Mark asked him to name the good things that Jacob had done to warrant God coming to Jacob and promising to be with him."

"Jacob had not done anything good."

"Exactly. I think for the first time Muhammad realized that it is not by our good actions but by God's plan that we can have a relationship with God." Stacey stared at the ground. "Maybe God is convicting him, and he is doing the only thing he knows how to do. I've heard of others doing that before." Marie nodded thoughtfully.

"That would make sense. I've caught him reading my Bible several times. He said he was preparing for his lesson with Mark, but that didn't make sense." Stacey rushed to her friend and took her hands in hers.

"Wouldn't it be wonderful if Muhammad accepted Christ?" Stacey asked. She dropped Marie's hands and added, "I know Mark is going through the stories with him, but he's only in the Old Testament. I don't think he'll get to the New Testament for a while."

"Muhammad has heard about Jesus many times but I have never seen him like this before. I had almost given up praying for him. He has always been so dismissive of my faith. Can't Mark just go ahead and do the stories from the New Testament?"

"I don't know," Stacey said. "We are so new to this storying thing." Stacey's face brightened. "It won't hurt to ask. I'll see what he says…"

As I packed my kitchen in preparation for our move from one West African country to another, I talked to the African woman leaning against the counter. She had bought a bookshelf from us and was waiting for the cart to arrive to pick it up. When I found out she was a Christian and attended a local church of another denomination, I began talking to her about storying as a witnessing tool. I told her the creation story as an example. "That was a great story," she said.

"Let me show you how to ask the questions," I replied. I began with the first question, "What are some things that God made?" She looked blank. I repeated the question.

"Everything," she finally said.

"What can we learn about God from the fact that He made all these things?"

She replied, "We need to follow Jesus and do good things." A good answer, but not one we find in the story. As I continued with the questions, her answers were the same – repetition of information she had memorized in church that had nothing to do with the story. It was clear that she had never learned the skill of gleaning truths from a Bible story. I thought of the baptism classes I had seen, where candidates sat with heads bowed as the leader talked about the information they needed to know before they could be baptized. I do not doubt that this woman in my kitchen believed in Jesus and had accepted Him as her Savior. If she had difficulty seeing elements of God's character through His act of creation, however, did she have difficulty recognizing God and His working in her own life?

Discipleship goes beyond learning information, beyond head knowledge. Discipleship is a journey of transformation where individuals are held accountable for the truths they are learning. Not only do we need to be transformed, but we need to disciple others and lead them to church. Healthy churches are composed of people who want to be transformed and who are transforming culture as they reach out and plant other churches. Accountability can be scary for those of us from an individualistic freedom-loving culture. The fear that our personal freedom may be restricted looms over us. As Christian leaders, are we willing to be accountable for the truths that we have learned? Are we holding new disciples accountable for the truths they learn?

Because CBS has been used for over 15 years in some places, it is possible to evaluate its effectiveness in bringing people to church. This chapter will discuss some of the challenges faced by users of CBS that have been revealed through the years and how those challenges might be addressed.

CBS and Challenges

In the fall of 2005, Grant Lovejoy challenged me to ask some essential questions about CBS in West Africa. Is CBS getting us to church? Is CBS getting us to reproducible church? I began asking those questions of myself and other storyers. I did not like what I discovered. On the one hand, I found abundant evidence that individuals were finding Christ because of CBS. But storying groups that turned into churches were rare. I discovered some possible reasons why it might be difficult for a storying group to turn into a church.

1. CBS is so subtle new believers do not know what happened to them. When someone in a storying group accepts Christ, family members are shocked that converts want to leave their religion to embrace a new one. The new believers do not know how to respond. They may say, "It's the truth," but without going through the stories, it is difficult for them to move beyond that. The beauty of CBS is that it confronts worldview barriers with truths from Scripture. But this breakdown can happen gradually over a long period of time. New believers often cannot easily explain what they believe to others or why they decided to accept Christ.

2. CBS is not easily reproducible. Although we encourage hearers to repeat the stories, unless special training is involved or the stories are recorded and available digitally, new nonliterate believers cannot easily reproduce the entire set of stories.

3. CBS primarily consists of head knowledge – discovering truths. New believers accept these truths. We have been remiss in helping converts to understand that discipleship goes beyond understanding truths to developing a living, daily, relationship with God. We do not always help new believers understand how the truths they are learning can be applied to their daily lives or help them tell their own faith stories.

4. We have become content to go slowly. We have too often gone ahead with our schedule (a story a week) rather than be sensitive to the spiritual needs of the people. The truth is that if the Spirit is moving and people are being convicted and we are not yet to the end of the Evangelism Track, we need to take them there as quickly as possible. We can always return and do the last stories in more depth. We want people to be interested in what will happen next. If they are only interested, we should continue as usual. However, if they are convicted, if the Holy Spirit is speaking to someone or several in a group, we should not make them wait.

5. We have not built in accountability from the beginning to "witness" to others, nor helped listeners understand what church looks like. We have not held the group accountable for sharing the stories with others each week.

6. By focusing on the stories, we have not helped the listeners see how the truths apply to their daily decisions. It can appear as if Christianity is a religion of "long ago."

7. Once we complete the Evangelism Track, we often switch to literate methods for discipleship of new believers. Because we are more comfortable with literacy and appreciate individualism and personal freedom, we may pull away or not be as available as we were during the Evangelism Track. We may leave groups with head knowledge instead of working to bring them to church.

8. At the same time, because it may take a long time to do the Evangelism Track, we can build such good relationships with the people that we become a part of their social network and dependency results. We may feel responsible if they are persecuted. They learn to depend upon us and may become content.

Does this mean we should not use Chronological Bible Storying? Not at all! The wondrous thing is, before storying, in some of our people groups, we did not have even individual believers. Now, through storying, we do! We must always be sensitive to the needs of oral learners. Oral methods and boldness are not mutually exclusive, however.

I now believe that CBS is most effective in these circumstances:

1. The listeners are not a transient population. The same group of people should be available to attend most of the storying sessions. It helps to meet at a time that best suits the needs of the listeners, not necessarily the needs of the storyer. In one situation, I storied every morning at 7:00 a.m. in one courtyard.

2. The listeners are confined in some way in that their circumstances require that they spend a specific amount of time in a given place. A tradition among many people groups is that widows must stay in their courtyards or even in their houses for several months following their husband's death. People may be confined to a hospital room because of an illness. In some cultures, women spend a lot of time in their homes because they are not allowed to travel alone in public. One of our most effective pastors in Mali became a believer in a storying group while he was in prison in another country. In situations where people are confined, if the storyer can gain access to them, the people may relish a distraction and be more open to listening to the stories. Once in the village, I visited a woman who was newly-widowed. Knowing tradition required that she spend about eight weeks in her courtyard, I asked if I could visit her daily and tell her stories from God's Word to "soothe her heart." She readily agreed. She and her household eventually became believers.

3. We do not limit ourselves to storying groups. In my later ministry, while we lived in the village, several individuals who would have been persecuted if they had been participated in one

of our groups knew they could stop by our house for one-on-one storying. In this situation, I did not emphasize learning the stories but rather went through them as quickly as possible. I relied on literacy for I kept a spreadsheet to show me where each person was in the storying track. I had printed out my stories and gathered them in a large black notebook. Someone, usually a woman who had told her family she was going to the market, would stop by my house and say she was ready for a story. I would whip out my book, see which story was next for her, familiarize myself with the story, and tell it to her, then go through the questions. After each story and questions, I would ask the listener if she wanted to hear another story. Sometimes they would say, "Hit me again," and I would tell another one. I let the listener determine how many stories I would tell, though rarely did I tell more than three at one time. Several people became believers through this process.

4. The people are hostile to the gospel. If by giving a gospel presentation, a barrier will be created which will keep you from having an opportunity to share again, then storying is a way to break through these barriers.

5. The people do not believe they are lost. They do not see a need for Christ. One of the beauties of storying is it gets people lost before it gets them saved.

6. Storying is a wonderful discipleship tool in the local church. CBS provides a biblical foundation for growth.

S-T4T

S-T4T (Storying Training for Trainers) is a church-planting strategy that largely responds to the concerns about Chronological Bible Storying getting to church. S-T4T also uses Bible stories but focuses on church planting from the beginning. In the resource section of this chapter is a link to the S-T4T website where you can download their training manual that was edited by Stephen Stringer. S-T4T has its roots in T4T, a globally effective, church-planting strategy.

The T4T website is available in the resource section. The concept of T4T is that from the beginning, believers are trained and held accountable for training others in evangelism and discipleship. It is a strategy of relationship-building, of encouraging believers, of being available. The missionary who developed it encouraged collectivistic values from the beginning. New believers are taught gospel truths and encouraged to share with others immediately what they have learned. They also share personal testimonies of the difference knowing Jesus is making in their lives. Rather than focus solely on head knowledge, T4T also focuses on accountability.

In my experience, when individuals with Western individualistic values meet T4T, they have difficulty understanding that for the strategy to be effective, leaders must invest themselves in the group. Those who do not share this collectivistic value of feeling a sense of duty to a group tend to look at T4T with different eyes. They may look for a church-planting formula, something they can "implement" and still enjoy personal freedom.

Perhaps because the developers of S-T4T understood our tendency to look for formulas, the S-T4T manual clearly states that S-T4T may not be effective in all situations. S-T4T combines the accountability of T4T with sharing truths with oral communicators through the use of faith stories and Bible stories.

The following is from page 9 of the S-T4T manual.

> S-T4T is…a systematic approach to evangelism and life-on-life discipleship that results in reproducing churches. It is not a series of lessons to be taught. It is a program in which believers meet regularly for fellowship, worship, accountability, and

discipleship. The discipleship portion of the S-T4T strategy covers the foundations of Christian life and discipleship found in the original T4T discipleship material, including 1) assurance of salvation; 2) prayer; 3) devotional life; 4) church; 5) the character and nature of God; and 6) widespread Gospel proclamation. These themes are integrated carefully and intentionally into the S-T4T strategy and core story set.

S-T4T is not chronological Bible storying. S-T4T uses a chronological approach to teaching the discipleship and church-planting lessons of T4T through Bible stories, but the evangelism strategy starts with personal testimonies, "hook" stories and a Gospel presentation using a brief biblical panorama that leads to a call for decision. Bible storying is the vehicle by which the T4T church-planting strategy conveys truth.

The editor of the S-T4T manual recently told me that when using the Jesus as sacrifice theme frequently presented in CBS, he found that listeners tend to think of sacrifice as ritual, far removed from themselves. In S-T4T, they begin where the people are by discussing their personal problems and how a personal relationship with Jesus can meet the people's needs. While being careful not to present a "prosperity gospel," from the beginning, leaders help the people understand what a personal relationship with Christ looks like in their daily lives. Listeners are held accountable for immediately applying the truths they are learning through the Bible stories.

Becoming Relational

I have said in the past that I do not know whether the main reason Chronological Bible Storying "works" is because it breaks down worldview barriers in the listeners or because it forces those of us with individualistic tendencies to be more relational. Perhaps, depending upon how it is implemented, CBS combines both worldview values. It is difficult to tell the Bible stories and lead a discussion time without mastering the language. It is difficult to master a language without being a learner among the people. When we meet regularly with the people to share stories, we learn more about them and invest in their lives. One observer who came to one of my groups where I was storying to a group of about five village women, noticed that as I sat on a stool, the women were crowded around me, touching me. One leaned against me with her elbows in my lap, as she cupped her chin, staring up at me as I shared the story. Though this kind of togetherness may not be appropriate in all cultures, in this group, even in 110 degree heat, being close was part of the storying experience. I realize now that such togetherness went against my natural tendencies in that whenever I finished the Evangelism Track and had new converts, I began distancing myself from the group, looking for places where I could share more stories, have more converts. I told myself I was being a good missionary by "moving on." But in retrospect, I believe I was relieved to no longer felt a sense of duty to the group. After all, they were now saved. I tried to do discipleship from arm's length, which is impossible. Perhaps I am more comfortable separating evangelism from the daily grind of discipleship because of my U.S. American individualistic values. I do not think that I am alone.

Conclusion

We cannot think, store information in memory, or even give something a name without resorting to a story. We see the world as it was depicted through the stories we heard from childhood. The stories we have heard have influenced our values, personalities, behavior, beliefs, and our communication style. We will repeat our cultural stories to others automatically unless we stop and think critically about our assumptions.

If not, we cannot help but interpret the world around us through the stories of our own culture.

When we encounter others who grew up listening to different stories, stories that emphasize the importance of duty to a group, for example, we have a choice. Rather than making judgements of superiority, we can grow to appreciate difference. God knit us individually in our mother's womb. Nothing is a surprise to Him, not our worldview, our culture, our personality, or our preferred form of communication. If we want to understand how much God appreciates difference, we only have to visit an aquarium.

From God's written Word, the Bible, we have the story of God working through history, working in individual's lives. How many of us could leave our homes and the familiar as Abraham was called to do? Sometimes, I asked new personnel if they discovered that the only way they could reach their people group would be to give up their U.S. American citizenship and become a citizen of a different country, would they be willing to do that. I asked that question to make them think, not because I thought it was a good idea. We often talk of our identity as being in Christ, but realistically, more often our identity is tied up with our passports. It is interesting that God created us with this need to identify with others and to share worldviews.

For some reason, God has chosen to work through us, even as restricted as we are by culture. As we share God's Word with others, may we also be willing to share our faith stories. Our story is unique. We are the main character in our story, but ultimately, the story is not about us. We must be willing to be transformed, to be obedient as God is bringing the world to Himself. For those of us whom God has called to share His Word with those who have never heard, we must be conscious that the stories we tell with our mouths and with our lives are stories that honor God. Our stories must reflect Him.

Mark didn't try to stop the tears that came to his eyes as Muhammad lifted his head.

"I can't believe it," Muhammad said. "All this time... Now I know what Marie has been talking about." Mark grasped Muhammad's arms, shaking him slightly.

"You are not only my friend, you are now my brother, my brother in Christ."

"I don't know what to say," Muhammad said.

"I'm so glad Stacey convinced me to go ahead and go over the stories in the New Testament quickly."

"Yes, I don't know what it is about those stories, but even though I've heard Marie talk many times about her faith, I never really knew what she meant." Muhammad paused, his eyes downcast. "I don't know what happens next. My uncle, the chief, is not going to be happy about this...you know they are going to blame you, don't you?" he asked.

"Muhammad, God knows what is going to happen. We don't. All we can do is be faithful and obedient to share about Him and what He is doing in our lives."

"I've never felt this way before," Muhammad said. "I can honestly say I am not worried."

"Good." Mark sat back on the couch and motioned for Muhammad to sit on the chair. "Can you tell me what just happened here?"

"Of course. I believe. I just accepted Christ as my Savior."

"Do you think you could share this with someone else who needs to accept Christ also?" Muhammad shook his head.

"I don't know about that."

"Who better to go and tell others? Remember the story of the demon-possessed man? Jesus told him to go and tell what had happened to him. Jesus wants us to tell others that they, too, can have a relationship with Him." Muhammad nodded. "This is good news. We need to share it."

"I suppose I could talk to Ali tonight, when he is alone after closing the store and before he heads home."

"Wonderful. Ali has heard many of the stories. I know he has been listening. We will pray that God intervenes to give you enough privacy to tell him about your decision."

Across the village, Stacey and Marie sat on a bench in Marie's courtyard. It was unusual for Stacey to visit her in the morning, but Mark had announced that he was going to do an overview of the New Testament stories and ask Muhammad to make a decision during their language time. Stacey had rushed to tell her friend, knowing that they needed to pray. Side by side they sat on the wooden bench, their hands clasped, their babies playing on the mat under the tree. Marie squeezed Stacey's hand. "God is good," she said.

"Yes," Stacey replied. "God is good."

Resources:

Bowers, C. A. (2005). The false promises of constructivist theories of learning: A global and ecological critique. New York, NY: Peter Lang Academic.

Bronfenbrenner, U. (1981). The ecology of human development: Experiments by nature and design. Cambridge, MA: Harvard University Press.

Brookfield, S. D. (2012). Teaching for critical thinking: Tools and techniques to help students question their assumptions. San Francisco: Jossey-Bass.

Chopra, P. (2004). Distorted mirrors: (de)centring images of the 'illiterate Indian village woman' through ethnographic research narratives. In A. Robinson-Pant (Ed.), Women, literacy, and development (pp. 35-56). New York, NY: Routledge.

Cole, M. (2005). Cross-cultural and historical perspectives on the developmental consequences of education. Human Development, 48, 195-216. doi: 10.1159/000086855

Dillon, C. (2012). Telling the gospel through story: Evangelism that keeps hearers Wanting More. Downers Grove, IN: InterVarsity.

Field, J. L. (1977). The learning efforts of Jamaican adults of low literacy attainment (Doctoral dissertation). Retrieved from ProQuest UMI dissertations publishing. (NK36646)

Gudykunst, W. B. (Ed.). (2005). Theorizing about intercultural communication. Thousand Oaks, CA: Sage.

Hofstede, G. (1980). Culture's consequences: International differences in work-related values. Beverly Hills, CA: Sage.

Howard, R. W. (1987). Concepts and schemata: An introduction. Philadelphia: Taylor & Francis.

International Orality Network, & Lausanne Committee for World Evangelization (ION, & LCWE). (2005). Making disciples of oral learners: To proclaim his story where it has not been known before. Lima, NY: International Orality Network.

Jabr, F. (2013). Why the brain prefers paper. Scientific American, 309, 48-53.

Jandt, F. E. (2004). An introduction to intercultural communication: Identities in a global community (4th ed.). Thousand Oaks, CA: Sage.

Knowles, M. S., Holton, E. F., & Swanson, R. A. (2012). The Adult Learner: The definitive classic in adult education and human resource development (7th ed.). New York, NY: Routledge.

Koehler, P. F. (2010). Telling God's story with power: Biblical storytelling in oral cultures. Pasadena, CA: William Carey Library.

Li, J. (2012). Cultural foundations of learning: East and west. New York, NY: Cambridge University Press.

Lingenfelter, J. E., & Lingenfelter, S. G. (2003). Teaching cross-culturally: An incarnational model for learning and teaching. Grand Rapids, MI: Baker Academic.

Mangen, A., Walgermo, B. R., & Bronnick, K. (2013). Reading linear texts on paper versus computer screen: Effects on reading comprehension. International Journal of Educational Research, 58, 61-68.

Maranz, D. (2001). African friends and money matters. Dallas, TX: SIL International.

Merriam, S. B., & Bierema, L. L. (2014). Adult learning: Linking theory and practice. San Francisco, CA: Jossey-Bass.

Nisbett, R. E. (2003). The geography of thought: How Asians and Westerners think differently…and why. New York, NY: Free Press.

Nishida, H. (2005). Cultural schema theory. In W. B. Gudykunst (Ed.), Theorizing about intercultural communication, 401-418. Thousand Oaks, CA: Sage.

Nussbaum, S. (2005). American cultural baggage: How to recognize and deal with it. Maryknoll, NY: Orbis.

Ong, W. J. (2002). Orality and literacy: The technologizing of the word. New York: Routledge.

Oyserman, D., Coon, H. M., & Kemmelmeier, M. (2002). Rethinking individualism and collectivism: Evaluation of theoretical assumptions and meta-analyses. Psychological Bulletin, 128, 3-72. doi: 10.1037//0033-2909.128.1.3

Sanchez, D. R., and Terry, J. O. (2009). LifeStory encounters. Fort Worth, TX: Church Starting Network.

Tian, J. (2010). A comparative study of Chinese and American cultural context and the influence on communication. Journal of Language Teaching and Research, 1, 524-526. doi:10.4304/jltr.1.4.524-526

Tiegreen, C. (2012). Story thru the Bible: An interactive way to connect to God's Word (Walk thru the Bible). Colorado Springs, CO: NavPress.

Terry, J. O. (2009). Basic Bible storying: Preparing and presenting Bible stories for evangelism, discipleship, training, and ministry. Fort Worth, TX: Church Starting Network.

_____. (2009). Death stories from the Bible. Fort Worth: Church Starting Network.

_____. (2009). Food stories from the Bible. Fort Worth: Church Starting Network.

_____. (2009). Grief stories from the Bible: Good news for those with stories of misfortune or grief. Fort Worth: Church Starting Network.

_____. (2008). Hope stories from the Bible. Fort Worth: Church Starting Network.

_____. (2009). Water stories from the Bible. Fort Worth: Church Starting Network.

Thompson, L. W. (2014, November). Teaching nonliterate adults: Insights from Illeris's

learning theory. Paper presented at the Commission for International Adult Education International Pre Conference (CIAE) to the 63rd American Association for Adult and Continuing Education (AAACE) Annual Conference, Charleston, SC. Available from ERIC.

Tobin, J. J., Wu, D. Y. H., & Davidson, D. H. (1989). Preschool in three cultures: Japan, China, and the United States. New Haven, CT: Yale University Press.

United Nations Educational, Scientific, and Cultural Organization (UNESCO). (2005a). "Aspect of literacy assessment. Topics and issues from the UNESCO expert meeting, June, 2003." Paris, France: UNESCO. Available from http://unesdoc.unesco.org/images/0014/001401/140125eo.pdf

Van Vreeswijk, M., Broersen, J., & Nadort, M. (Eds.). (2012). The Wiley-Blackwell handbook of schema therapy: Theory, research and practice (Wiley Clinical Psychology Handbooks, 1st ed.). West Sussex, United Kingdom: John Wiley & Sons.

Willis, A. T., & Snowden, M. (2010). Truth that sticks: How to communicate Velcro truth in a Teflon world. Colorado Springs, CO: NavPress.

WEBSITES:

Communication Across Barriers:
http://www.combarriers.com/CommunicationStyles

Faith Comes By Hearing:
https://www.faithcomesbyhearing.com

Global Recordings Network:
http://globalrecordings.net/en

God's Story Project:
http://www.gods-story.org

IndigiTube:
http://www.indigitube.tv

International Orality Network (ION):
http://www.orality.net

Man of Peace Film:
http://www.manofpeace-thefilm.org

OneStory Partnership:
http://onestory.org

Orality Strategies (IMB):
https://oralitystrategies.org

Renew: Reaching the Remote:
http://www.renewoutreach.com

Scriptures in Use:
http://www.siutraining.org

Simply the Story (STS):
http://simplythestory.org/oralbiblestories

S-T4T:
http://www.st4t.org

Story for All (Story4All): Truth that Sticks:
http://story4all.com/index.shtml

Story Runners (Campus Crusade):
http://storyrunners.org

Storying the Scriptures: Telling the Gospel through Story:
http://storyingthescriptures.com

T4Global: Communicating Truth to Oral Learners:
http://t4global.org

T4T:
http://t4tonline.org/

Truth Sticks (Mark Snowden):
https://truthsticks.wordpress.com/author/wmarksnowden/